Math Made Easy

10 Minutes A Day

Decimals

D1194293

4th Grade Math Workbook

Author Sean McArdle
Consultant Alison Tribley

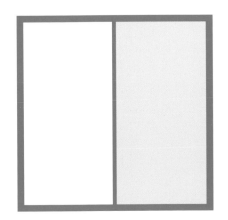
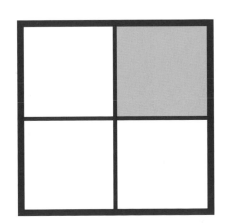
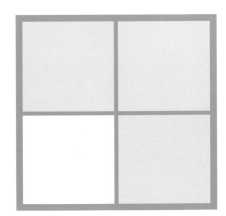

DK

This timer counts up to 10 minutes.
When it reaches 10:00 it will beep.

How to use the timer:

Switch the timer ON.
Press the triangle ▶ to START the timer.
Press the square ■ to STOP or PAUSE the timer.
Press the square ■ to RESET the timer to 00:00.
Press any button to WAKE UP the timer.

Penguin
Random
House

Editors Jolyon Goddard,
Nishtha Kapil, Allison Singer
Educational Consultant Alison Tribley
Art Editor Jyotsna Julka
Managing Editor Soma B. Chowdhury
Managing Art Editors Richard Czapnik,
Ahlawat Gunjan
Producer, Pre-Production Francesca Wardell
Producer Christine Ni
Math Consultant Sean McArdle
DTP Designer Anita Yadav

First American Edition, 2015
Published in the United States by DK Publishing
345 Hudson Street, New York, New York 10014

Copyright © 2015 Dorling Kindersley Limited
A Penguin Random House Company
10 9 8 7 6 5 4 3 2 1
001–273223–Jan/2015

A catalog record for this book
is available from the Library of Congress.
ISBN 978-1-4654-2823-3

DK books are available at special discounts when purchased
in bulk for sales promotions, premiums, fund-raising, or
educational use. For details, contact: DK Publishing Special
Markets, 345 Hudson Street, New York, New York 10014
SpecialSales@dk.com

Printed and bound in China by L. Rex Printing Co. Ltd.
Timer designed and made in Hong Kong by Tritech

All images © Dorling Kindersley Limited
For further information see: www.dkimages.com

A WORLD OF IDEAS:
SEE ALL THERE IS TO KNOW

Contents

Time Taken

Time Filler:
In these boxes are some extra challenges to extend your skills. You can do them if you have some time left after finishing the questions and continue until you hear the 10-minute beep. Or, these can be stand-alone activities that you can do in 10 minutes.

Equivalents 1

4

Just like fractions, decimal numbers can be used to show the proportion of a whole. Remember: $\frac{1}{2} = 0.5$, $\frac{1}{4} = 0.25$, and so on.

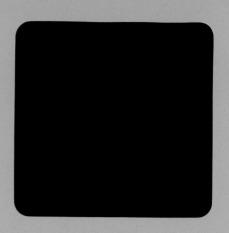

1 Shade in 0.5 of each shape.

2 Shade in 0.25 of each shape.

3 Shade in 0.75 of each shape.

4 Write each decimal as a fraction.

0.5 $\frac{\Box}{\Box}$ 0.25 $\frac{\Box}{\Box}$ 0.75 $\frac{\Box}{\Box}$

5 Draw lines linking each decimal amount to the shape with the equivalent area shaded.

0.5

0.25

0.75

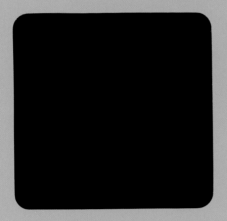

Time Filler:
Look at questions 6 and 7 again. What decimal amount has been left unshaded? Do you have a chessboard? What decimal amount of the squares is black? What decimal amount is white?

(6) What decimal amount of each shape has been shaded?

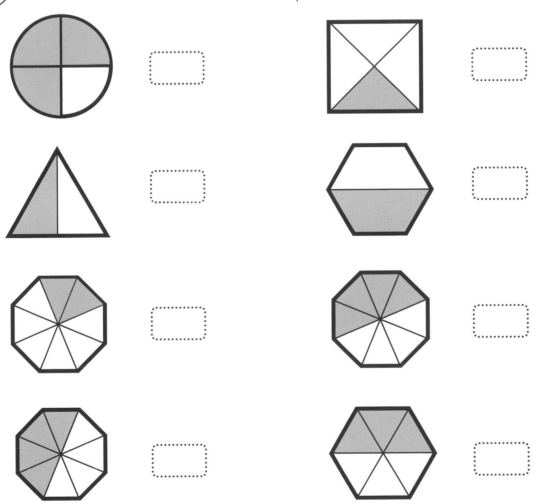

(7) Write the corresponding decimal for each shaded portion.

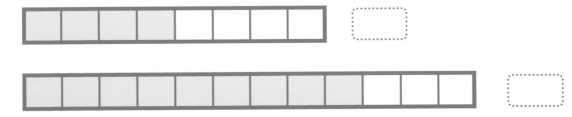

Equivalents 2

Fractions can also be written as decimals, and decimals can be written as fractions.

1 Write each fraction as a decimal.

$\frac{1}{10}$ ☐ $\frac{1}{100}$ ☐ $\frac{3}{10}$ ☐ $\frac{7}{100}$ ☐

$\frac{6}{10}$ ☐ $\frac{9}{10}$ ☐ $\frac{3}{100}$ ☐ $\frac{9}{100}$ ☐

$\frac{6}{100}$ ☐ $\frac{5}{10}$ ☐ $\frac{8}{100}$ ☐ $\frac{2}{100}$ ☐

$\frac{2}{10}$ ☐ $\frac{4}{10}$ ☐ $\frac{7}{10}$ ☐ $\frac{4}{100}$ ☐

$\frac{12}{10}$ ☐ $\frac{68}{100}$ ☐ $\frac{23}{100}$ ☐ $\frac{10}{100}$ ☐

$\frac{45}{10}$ ☐ $\frac{32}{100}$ ☐ $\frac{51}{10}$ ☐ $\frac{97}{100}$ ☐

$\frac{61}{100}$ ☐ $\frac{18}{10}$ ☐ $\frac{33}{10}$ ☐ $\frac{75}{100}$ ☐

$\frac{28}{10}$ ☐ $\frac{87}{10}$ ☐ $\frac{66}{100}$ ☐ $\frac{22}{100}$ ☐

$\frac{52}{100}$ ☐ $\frac{19}{10}$ ☐ $\frac{73}{100}$ ☐ $\frac{92}{10}$ ☐

Time Filler:
Think of ten numbers between 1 and 99. Write each of these numbers as the numerator (top number) in a fraction, with 10 as the denominator (lower number), and then again with 100 as the denominator. Now write these 20 fractions as their equivalent decimals.

② Write each decimal as a fraction.

0.08 ⬜/⬜   0.15 ⬜/⬜   0.06 ⬜/⬜   0.27 ⬜/⬜   0.9 ⬜/⬜

0.34 ⬜/⬜   0.57 ⬜/⬜   0.05 ⬜/⬜   0.97 ⬜/⬜   0.02 ⬜/⬜

0.62 ⬜/⬜   0.48 ⬜/⬜   0.23 ⬜/⬜   0.71 ⬜/⬜   0.6 ⬜/⬜

0.01 ⬜/⬜   0.1 ⬜/⬜   0.5 ⬜/⬜   0.68 ⬜/⬜   0.7 ⬜/⬜

0.25 ⬜/⬜   0.75 ⬜/⬜   0.3 ⬜/⬜   0.03 ⬜/⬜   0.8 ⬜/⬜

Dividing by 10 and 100

The word *decimal* comes from the Latin word *decimus*, meaning "tenth." Can you see why?

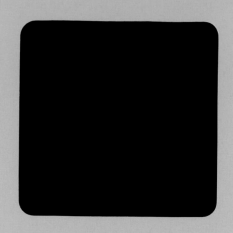

(1) Write whether 1 is in the tens, ones, tenths, or hundredths place.

1.0	0.1	0.01	2.1	32.01
....	....	....	....	....

4.12	21.8	7.1	1.2	10.6
....	....	....	....	....

(2) Suki has a total of $13.68 in her piggy bank. Which part of that number is the ones place and which is the tenths place?

Ones [ ]

Tenths [ ]

(3) Divide each number by 10 and write the answer in the decimal form.

50 [ ]	4 [ ]	81 [ ]	70 [ ]	25 [ ]
7 [ ]	35 [ ]	60 [ ]	90 [ ]	5 [ ]
15 [ ]	11 [ ]	18 [ ]	20 [ ]	32 [ ]

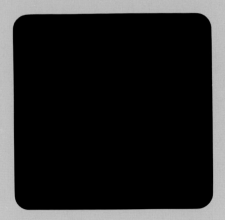

Time Filler:
Write the ages of everyone in your family. Divide each of their ages by ten. Then repeat the exercise, this time dividing their ages by 100. Write your answers in decimal amounts.

④ Divide each number by 100 and write the answer in the decimal form.

78 [ ]   12 [ ]   43 [ ]   9 [ ]   99 [ ]

40 [ ]   5 [ ]   66 [ ]   1 [ ]   50 [ ]

32 [ ]   10 [ ]   70 [ ]   55 [ ]   92 [ ]

⑤ Write whether 5 is in the tens, ones, tenths, or hundredths place.

56.3   7.05   0.5   5.62   0.05

....

15.2   12.5   51.9   20.5   5.78

....

⑥ Write whether 8 is in the tens, ones, tenths, or hundredths place.

7.68   8.6   9.83   12.08   8.43

....

4.81   10.8   8.24   6.38   18.5

....

Rounding Decimals

When rounding, always remember that decimal numbers ending in .5 should be rounded upward, not downward.

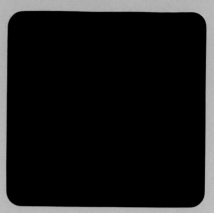

① Round each decimal to the nearest whole number.

6.3 [   ]   7.6 [   ]   9.8 [   ]

4.2 [   ]   0.5 [   ]   24.5 [   ]

24.9 [   ]   15.5 [   ]   15.7 [   ]

42.5 [   ]   12.1 [   ]   49.8 [   ]

18.2 [   ]   56.4 [   ]   79.5 [   ]

17.3 [   ]   89.5 [   ]   57.7 [   ]

93.9 [   ]   69.9 [   ]   87.9 [   ]

88.4 [   ]   88.5 [   ]   88.6 [   ]

68.5 [   ]   85.6 [   ]   65.8 [   ]

32.7 [   ]   73.3 [   ]   88.8 [   ]

90.5 [   ]   42.6 [   ]   59.1 [   ]

40.5 [   ]   52.5 [   ]   73.4 [   ]

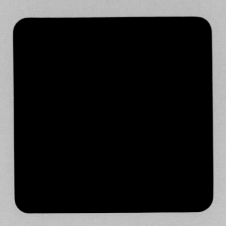

Time Filler:
Find two of your favorite books. Measure the length, width, and depth (thickness) of each book as accurately as possible with a ruler. Now round these numbers to the nearest inch.

2 Round each decimal to the nearest whole unit.

4.5 in	3.8 m	7.1 km
56.4 g	2.3 mi	12.5 g
66.6 m	86.5 ft	42.8 lb
47.6 ft	17.3 cm	19.1 km
15.5 cm	81.7 mm	23.7 kg
14.2 g	56.5 m	68.8 mi
49.2 ft	35.7 in	26.6 mm
76.4 m	76.5 cm	76.6 ft
67.5 g	57.2 lb	57.7 km

3 Caleb's favorite book is 8.2 in wide, 10.5 in long, and 0.7 in thick. Round these measurements to the nearest inch.

Comparing Decimals 1

Is there a point to decimal numbers?
Yes—it's called the decimal point!

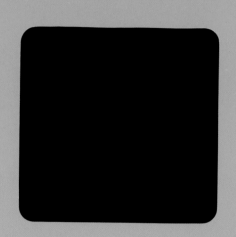

1 Circle the larger number in each pair.

3.6 6.3	4.8 8.4	3.5 3.8	9.0 8.9
5.3 4.9	8.0 6.9	12.3 13.3	23.3 33.2
21.2 22.1	35.8 58.3	18.6 16.8	31.5 35.1
2.9 9.2	1.5 2.5	19.8 18.9	34.1 33.9
80.1 80.9	26.3 23.6	14.7 17.4	55.4 54.5

2 Circle the smallest number in each group.

23.2   22.3   23.3   48.7   47.8   48.8   54.6   56.4   54.5

3 Circle the largest number in each group.

28.3   23.8   28.2   95.5   59.5   55.9   63.4   64.3   63.2

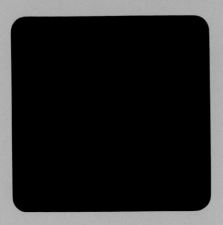

Time Filler:
Find six objects in the kitchen, such as a cup, small bowl, fork, spoon, potato, apple, etc. Pair up those of a similar size. Measure each item using a ruler and write the lengths, with the pairs together. Now circle the shorter length in each pair.

(4) Circle the smaller amount in each pair.

24.6 mm 26.4 mm	$2.58 $2.85	17.9 ft 19.7 ft
5.48 in 5.84 in	17.25 cm 12.75 cm	24.82 g 28.42 g
0.67 g 0.76 g	1.89 in 1.98 in	3.83 oz 3.38 oz
29.4 cm 49.2 cm	34.3 mi 33.4 mi	97.8 g 98.7 g
2.41 oz 4.21 oz	0.58 in 1.29 in	9.09 g 9.13 g

(5) Circle the larger amount in each pair.

8.09 g 8.9 g	8.8 in 0.65 in	0.56 cm 1.01 cm

(6) Circle the smallest amount in each group.

18.06 mi 18.04 mi 18.1 mi	36.67 kg 37.67 kg 36.66 kg

Measurements and Money

We use decimal numbers all the time. Weights, lengths, and amounts of money are often written as decimals.

1 Alex runs 1.82 mi, Mike runs 1.28 mi, and Harris runs 1.56 mi. Who runs farther than Harris?

....

2 Answer these questions.

How much longer is 1.45 m than 1.35 m?

Which weighs more, 2.56 kg or 2.65 kg?

Which of these measurements is the same as 108 cm?

10.8 m   1.8 m   1.08 m

3 Clara has 0.4 lb of fruit; Katie has double that amount. How much fruit does Katie have?

David has half Clara's amount. How much fruit does David have?

4 Rosie believes 186 cm is the same as 1.86 m. Is she correct?

Olly says 190 cm is 10 cm less than 2 m. Is he correct?

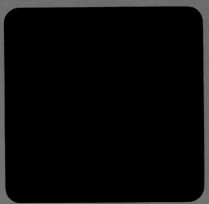

Time Filler:
Empty your piggy bank or money jar. Put all the different coins—pennies, nickels, dimes, etc.—into separate piles. How much is each pile worth? Write your answers in the decimal format (for example, $0.67) and add them all together. How much money do you have in total?

(5) Write each amount in cents (¢).

$3.50 $2.28 $0.67 $10.40

$1.45 $1.54 $4.51 $5.14

(6) Write each amount as dollars.

467 ¢   273 ¢   95 ¢   608 ¢

384 ¢   529 ¢   77 ¢   999 ¢

(7) What is three-quarters ($\frac{3}{4}$) of each amount? Give your answers in dollars.

$4 $1 $10 $8

(8) Gary's pencil is 4.98 in long, Larry's pencil is 4.94 in long, and Harry's pencil is 4.96 in long. Who has the shortest pencil?

Equivalents 3

They will look different, but many decimals can also be written as fractions.

Place each of these fractions in the correct place on the number lines.

(1) $\frac{4}{10}$ $\frac{6}{10}$ $\frac{2}{10}$

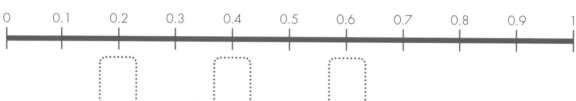

(2) $\frac{3}{10}$ $\frac{5}{10}$ $\frac{9}{10}$

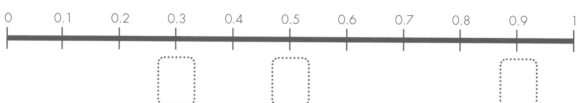

(3) $\frac{7}{10}$ $\frac{1}{10}$ $\frac{8}{10}$

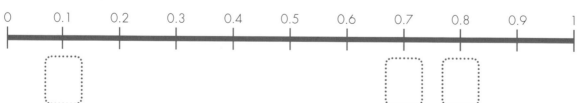

(4) $\frac{4}{5}$ $\frac{3}{5}$ $\frac{1}{5}$

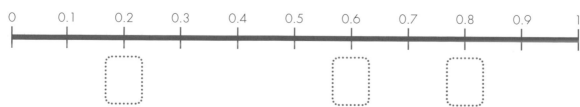

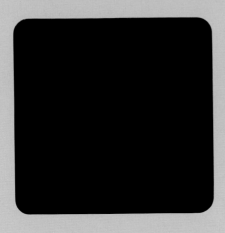

Time Filler:
Using a ruler, draw a 10-cm line and make a mark at the 0.5 (halfway) position along its length. Then, draw a 20-cm line and make marks at the 0.25, 0.5, and 0.75 positions. Last, draw a 30-cm line and make marks at the 0.1, 0.4, 0.6, and 0.9 positions.

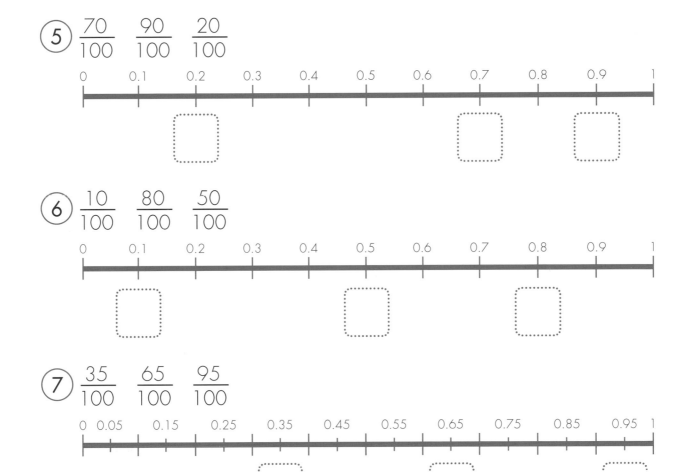

(5) $\dfrac{70}{100}$ $\dfrac{90}{100}$ $\dfrac{20}{100}$

0   0.1   0.2   0.3   0.4   0.5   0.6   0.7   0.8   0.9   1

(6) $\dfrac{10}{100}$ $\dfrac{80}{100}$ $\dfrac{50}{100}$

0   0.1   0.2   0.3   0.4   0.5   0.6   0.7   0.8   0.9   1

(7) $\dfrac{35}{100}$ $\dfrac{65}{100}$ $\dfrac{95}{100}$

0   0.05   0.15   0.25   0.35   0.45   0.55   0.65   0.75   0.85   0.95   1

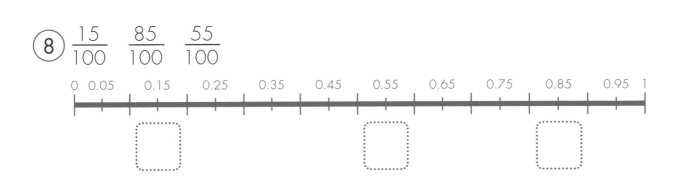

(8) $\dfrac{15}{100}$ $\dfrac{85}{100}$ $\dfrac{55}{100}$

0   0.05   0.15   0.25   0.35   0.45   0.55   0.65   0.75   0.85   0.95   1

Equivalents 4

Which do you prefer, fractions or decimals? Let's practice them both!

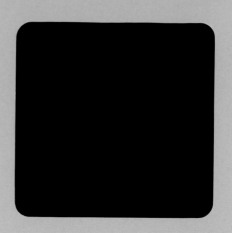

① Write each fraction in its decimal form.

$\dfrac{345}{1,000}$ [____] $\dfrac{250}{1,000}$ [____] $\dfrac{476}{1,000}$ [____] $\dfrac{132}{1,000}$ [____]

$\dfrac{781}{1,000}$ [____] $\dfrac{908}{1,000}$ [____] $\dfrac{285}{1,000}$ [____] $\dfrac{719}{1,000}$ [____]

$\dfrac{46}{1,000}$ [____] $\dfrac{83}{1,000}$ [____] $\dfrac{98}{1,000}$ [____] $\dfrac{66}{1,000}$ [____]

$\dfrac{51}{1,000}$ [____] $\dfrac{90}{1,000}$ [____] $\dfrac{81}{1,000}$ [____] $\dfrac{75}{1,000}$ [____]

$\dfrac{10}{1,000}$ [____] $\dfrac{5}{1,000}$ [____] $\dfrac{20}{1,000}$ [____] $\dfrac{1}{1,000}$ [____]

$\dfrac{29}{1,000}$ [____] $\dfrac{459}{1,000}$ [____] $\dfrac{205}{1,000}$ [____] $\dfrac{853}{1,000}$ [____]

$\dfrac{231}{1,000}$ [____] $\dfrac{85}{1,000}$ [____] $\dfrac{397}{1,000}$ [____] $\dfrac{59}{1,000}$ [____]

$\dfrac{109}{1,000}$ [____] $\dfrac{27}{1,000}$ [____] $\dfrac{720}{1,000}$ [____] $\dfrac{18}{1,000}$ [____]

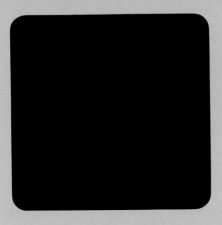

Time Filler:
Here is some extra practice with units:
How many meters (m) are there in one
kilometer (km)? How many centimeters
(cm) are there in 1 km? And how many
millimeters (mm) are there in 1 km?

② Write each decimal as a fraction.

0.645 ▭/▭   0.629 ▭/▭   0.173 ▭/▭   0.615 ▭/▭

0.03 ▭/▭   0.004 ▭/▭   0.6 ▭/▭   0.07 ▭/▭

0.19 ▭/▭   0.001 ▭/▭   0.429 ▭/▭   0.8 ▭/▭

③ How much is 0.01 of 1 km? Answer in meters. ▭

How much is 0.001 of 1 kg? Answer in grams. ▭

④ How much is 0.01 of 1 l? Answer in milliliters.

▭

How much is 0.001 of 10 km? Answer in meters.

▭

Beat the Clock 1

Test your decimals knowledge.
Start your 10-minute timer now!

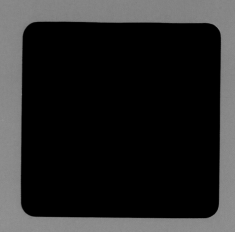

Write each fraction in its decimal form.

① $\frac{1}{4}$ [　　　]　　② $\frac{3}{4}$ [　　　]　　③ $\frac{1}{2}$ [　　　]

④ $\frac{2}{5}$ [　　　]　　⑤ $\frac{4}{5}$ [　　　]　　⑥ $\frac{1}{5}$ [　　　]

⑦ $\frac{3}{5}$ [　　　]　　⑧ $\frac{9}{10}$ [　　　]　　⑨ $\frac{1}{10}$ [　　　]

⑩ $\frac{7}{10}$ [　　　]　　⑪ $\frac{4}{10}$ [　　　]　　⑫ $\frac{5}{10}$ [　　　]

⑬ $\frac{6}{10}$ [　　　]　　⑭ $\frac{8}{10}$ [　　　]　　⑮ $\frac{3}{10}$ [　　　]

Divide each number by 10.

⑯ 7 [　　　]　　⑰ 18 [　　　]　　⑱ 12 [　　　]

⑲ 21 [　　　]　　⑳ 2 [　　　]　　㉑ 5 [　　　]

㉒ 11 [　　　]　　㉓ 30 [　　　]　　㉔ 50 [　　　]

㉕ 6 [　　　]　　㉖ 400 [　　　]　　㉗ 150 [　　　]

㉘ 360 [　　　]　　㉙ 700 [　　　]　　㉚ 490 [　　　]

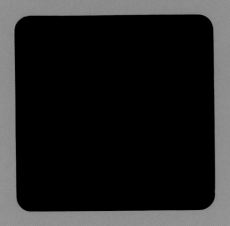

Time Filler:
Can you write $\frac{1}{8}$ as a decimal?
Now see if you can write $\frac{3}{8}$, $\frac{5}{8}$, and $\frac{7}{8}$ as decimals, too.

Round each number to the hundredths place (two decimal places).

(31) 5.671 [   ]　(32) 4.968 [   ]　(33) 1.635 [   ]

(34) 8.524 [   ]　(35) 12.965 [   ]　(36) 1.345 [   ]

(37) 8.046 [   ]　(38) 9.432 [   ]　(39) 0.657 [   ]

Round each number to the nearest whole number.

(40) 6.8 [   ]　(41) 7.9 [   ]　(42) 3.1 [   ]

(43) 7.5 [   ]　(44) 8.3 [   ]　(45) 9.7 [   ]

(46) 21.5 [   ]　(47) 36.5 [   ]　(48) 3.6 [   ]

Write each decimal as a fraction.

(49) 0.75 [   ]　(50) 0.96 [   ]　(51) 0.02 [   ]

(52) 0.25 [   ]　(53) 0.675 [   ]　(54) 0.008 [   ]

(55) 0.30 [   ]　(56) 0.003 [   ]　(57) 0.5 [   ]

Addition 1

Don't forget to include the number after the decimal point (the tenths place) when doing these equations.

1 Find the totals.

$3 + 1.5 =$ [ ]

$5 + 2.5 =$ [ ]

$8.3 + 4 =$ [ ]

$6.4 + 5 =$ [ ]

$7 + 0.2 =$ [ ]

$1 + 1.4 =$ [ ]

$6.9 + 3 =$ [ ]

$5 + 2.2 =$ [ ]

$7.4 + 3 =$ [ ]

$12.3 + 8 =$ [ ]

$2.4 + 6 =$ [ ]

$4.4 + 6 =$ [ ]

$12 + 8.6 =$ [ ]

$17.4 + 3 =$ [ ]

$18.7 + 6 =$ [ ]

$7.3 + 7 =$ [ ]

$14 + 0.7 =$ [ ]

$24 + 0.3 =$ [ ]

2 On vacation, Richard spent 3 days in France, 0.5 days in Luxembourg, 2.5 days in Belgium, and 3.5 days in the Netherlands, then returned home. How long was Richard's trip?

 days

③ Find the totals.

$3 + 4.6 + 2 =$ ⬚ $1.2 + 3 + 5 =$ ⬚

$6 + 8 + 3.5 =$ ⬚ $6 + 4 + 0.1 =$ ⬚

$6.3 + 4 + 4 =$ ⬚ $4.5 + 6 + 3 =$ ⬚

$8 + 3.9 + 3 =$ ⬚ $7.9 + 1 + 3 =$ ⬚

$4.6 + 4 + 6 =$ ⬚ $0.9 + 1 + 7 =$ ⬚

$9.1 + 9 + 2 =$ ⬚ $0.6 + 4 + 5 =$ ⬚

$3.4 + 5 + 6 =$ ⬚ $8 + 9 + 5.4 =$ ⬚

$7 + 6.3 + 4 =$ ⬚ $6.6 + 6 + 6 =$ ⬚

$6 + 4.3 + 12 =$ ⬚ $5.1 + 9 + 3 =$ ⬚

$4.8 + 6 + 9 =$ ⬚ $17 + 3 + 0.2 =$ ⬚

$7 + 2.2 + 8 =$ ⬚ $12 + 7 + 5.9 =$ ⬚

$4 + 7 + 6.9 =$ ⬚ $24 + 8 + 0.8 =$ ⬚

Addition 2

Don't be scared of the decimal point!
It's there to help you write numbers as
accurately as possible.

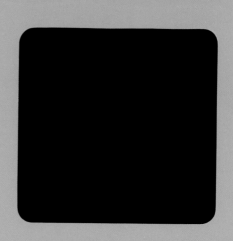

① Write the answers.

2.5 ft + 4 ft = [ ]

5.9 g + 7 g = [ ]

17 ft + 2.8 ft = [ ]

7 ft + 4.3 ft = [ ]

4.3 g + 9.4 g = [ ]

9.5 g + 5 g = [ ]

6.2 g + 4.1 g = [ ]

1.8 kg + 3 kg = [ ]

7.1 m + 3.4 m = [ ]

6.5 g + 4.4 g = [ ]

3 mi + 4.2 mi = [ ]

8 ft + 3.4 ft = [ ]

12 in + 4.8 in = [ ]

12.5 g + 3.4 g = [ ]

6.3 kg + 9.6 kg = [ ]

8.5 ml + 6.3 ml = [ ]

8 lb + 2.4 lb = [ ]

3.7 ml + 2.2 ml = [ ]

② Kim and Harry plant some flowers in
their garden. They plant 2.75 ft² with
roses and 1.75 ft² with daisies.
What is the total area they
planted with flowers?

[ ]

Time Filler:
Use the digits in your friends and
family members' birthdays to create
decimals, then add them together.
Try to make up ten problems to solve.

③ Martin needs $25.75 for a new bicycle tire.
He does a few odd jobs for family and neighbors
and earns $8.15, $5.20, $3.23, and $9.50.
How much money does Martin have now?

Does he have enough money to buy a new tire? _____

④ Find the total amounts.

$2.56 + $2.56 = ☐ $1.62 + $0.20 = ☐

$4.20 + $0.50 = ☐ $6.50 + $1.30 = ☐

$6.75 + $0.20 = ☐ $8.66 + $1.10 = ☐

$3.33 + $2.60 = ☐ $5.50 + $3.25 = ☐

$6.20 + $3.75 = ☐ $8.10 + $2.25 = ☐

$5.35 + $4.25 = ☐ $7.50 + $5.15 = ☐

$3.00 + $2.50 + $1.30 = ☐ $6.10 + $2.30 + $1.25 = ☐

$0.25 + $0.25 + $0.25 = ☐ $1.23 + $4.00 + $3.20 = ☐

$1.08 + $2.03 + $6.00 = ☐ $1.90 + $3.00 + $2.10 = ☐

Comparing Decimals 2

When comparing decimal numbers, read them very carefully. For example, 2.333 is just one-thousandth smaller than 2.334.

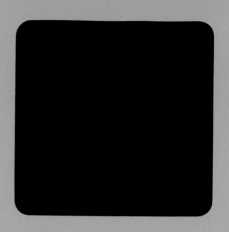

1 Circle the larger number in each pair.

| 3.6   1.9 | 5.86   5.68 | 7.674 7.688 | 1.03   1.003 |

2 Circle the smaller number in each pair.

| 2.05   2.48 | 3.867 3.847 | 5.231 4.999 | 5.051 5.105 |

3 Rewrite each row in order, starting with the smallest number.

| 3.756 | 3.75 | 3.675 | 3.57 |

| 4.086 | 4.085 | 4.058 | 4.068 |

| 12.3 | 11.9 | 13.867 | 11.444 |

| 8.23 | 3.82 | 2.83 | 3.28 |

Time Filler:
Using a tape measure, measure your height and the heights of two of your friends or family members. Measure to the nearest inch if possible. Then write the heights in order, with the tallest first.

(4) Circle the larger amount in each pair.

| 6.72 in   6.27 in | 4.88 g   4.91 g | 6.03 m   3.6 m |

(5) Circle the smaller amount in each pair.

| 8.326 mi   8.623 mi | 4.845 km 3.999 km | 5.123 ft   5.104 ft |

(6) Rewrite each row in order, starting with the largest amount.

| 4.867 mi | 4.881 mi | 6.496 mi | 4.904 mi |

....

| 18.826 kg | 12.978 kg | 31.423 kg | 31.4 kg |

....

| $7.49 | $7.40 | $8.00 | $7.94 |

....

| $15.67 | $18.23 | $15.76 | $17.78 |

....

Addition 3

How quickly can you solve these problems?
Concentrate, and... go!

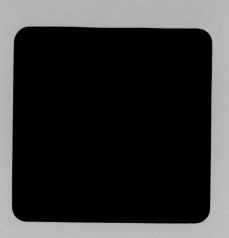

(1) Add the numbers.

$3.6 + 2.8 =$ [ ] $4.4 + 9.3 =$ [ ] $7.6 + 2.9 =$ [ ]

$6.25 + 4.4 =$ [ ] $4.4 + 18.3 =$ [ ] $7.2 + 11.2 =$ [ ]

$3.71 + 8.81 =$ [ ] $4.55 + 1.25 =$ [ ] $3.05 + 2.05 =$ [ ]

$8.92 + 4.19 =$ [ ] $3.85 + 1.05 =$ [ ] $12.3 + 3.8 =$ [ ]

$6.12 + 2.08 =$ [ ] $13.7 + 2.4 =$ [ ] $29.5 + 6.2 =$ [ ]

(2) Find the totals.

$3.0 + 6.1 + 7.3 =$ [ ] $7.3 + 2.4 + 1.6 =$ [ ]

$5.4 + 3.2 + 1.0 =$ [ ] $2.8 + 6.5 + 3.2 =$ [ ]

$6.7 + 3.9 + 4.9 =$ [ ] $8.2 + 5.0 + 3.8 =$ [ ]

$4.9 + 8.8 + 1.4 =$ [ ] $6.5 + 4.5 + 3.5 =$ [ ]

$12.2 + 4.4 + 10.0 =$ [ ] $13.2 + 5.5 + 12.6 =$ [ ]

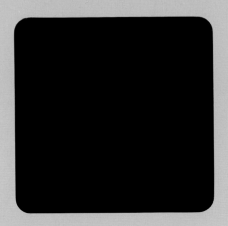

(3) Solve these problems.

4.6 + 3.4	5.6 + 6.8	7.1 + 3.4	9.3 + 1.4	6.1 + 4.8
12.8 + 6.7	11.6 + 4.7	15.3 + 2.9	24.7 + 3.3	64.8 + 7.4
4.63 + 1.27	5.89 + 2.33	1.07 + 2.46	4.36 + 1.44	8.26 + 1.74
60.34 + 31.47	31.23 + 14.56	56.12 + 21.08	23.99 + 12.01	33.93 + 83.72

(4) Each morning, Zara and Kyle walk 0.22 mi to the bus stop, travel 2.39 mi on the bus, and then walk 0.16 mi to reach their school. How far is their journey?

Addition 4

Pay close attention to place value
when solving these problems,
and make sure to double-check
your work!

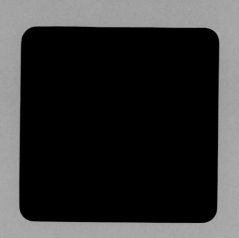

---

(1) Find the totals.

$3.48 + 5.52 =$ [   ] $1.09 + 0.91 =$ [   ]

$3.0 + 6.464 =$ [   ] $4.89 + 2.11 =$ [   ]

$6.042 + 1.1 =$ [   ] $5.109 + 7.9 =$ [   ]

$5.64 + 2.364 =$ [   ] $2.34 + 4.001 =$ [   ]

$7.25 + 3.593 =$ [   ] $7.62 + 3.041 =$ [   ]

---

(2) Solve these addition problems.

```
   2.65        1.783        6.20         9.132        2.391
+  1.46      + 2.620      + 3.88       + 1.410      + 0.129
---------    ---------    ---------    ---------    ---------
.........    .........    .........    .........    .........


  52.60       81.230       56.902        7.008        4.150
+  8.23      +  3.284     + 6.700      + 0.830      + 1.213
---------    ---------    ---------    ---------    ---------
.........    .........    .........    .........    .........


  23.600       0.600       12.850        4.94         6.403
+  0.123     + 3.567      + 9.006      + 0.70       + 4.892
---------    ---------    ---------    ---------    ---------
.........    .........    .........    .........    .........
```

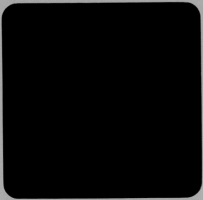

Time Filler:
Use a ruler to measure the lengths of the fingers and thumb on one of your hands to the nearest millimeter. Add the lengths together and write your answer in centimeters.

(3) Answer these questions.

How much is $3.56 plus $2.99?

What is 1.56 yd added to 1.86 yd?

How much is 1.675 mi increased by 0.255 mi?

What amount is $2.67 more than $12.50?

(4) A kitchen counter is made up of two pieces. One piece is 5.395 ft long and the other 1.746 ft. What will be the length of the whole counter when the two pieces are joined together?

(5) What is the total when $2.85 is added to each of these?

$2.69 $4.50

(6) Add this group of numbers and write the total.

2.455   7.234   8.167

Addition 5

Try these equations. They are slightly harder. You can still do them!

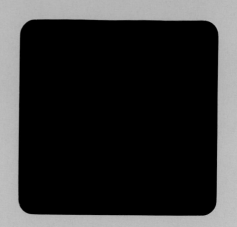

1 A car makes three journeys. The first journey is 8.627 mi, the second is 9.348 mi, and the third is 12.450 mi. How far does the car travel in total?

2 Write the answers.

2.423 + 1.534	1.867 + 2.427	0.655 + 2.809	7.291 + 0.810
0.836 + 6.190	2.056 + 1.006	7.340 + 8.455	4.980 + 2.713
4.006 + 1.040	3.501 + 0.660	2.956 + 0.300	12.535 + 6.375
10.044 2.860 + 8.009	12.800 0.640 + 4.235	6.834 1.423 + 0.223	9.471 1.250 + 3.089

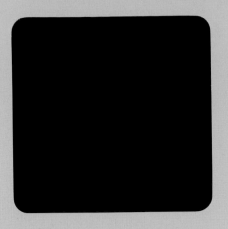

Time Filler:
Here's an extra question. At lunch, Nate spent $3.25 on a sandwich, $1.30 on a drink, $0.65 on a snack, and $0.42 on an apple. How much did he spend in total?

3) Find the totals.

$4.6 + 3.4 =$ ☐ $6.6 + 3.9 =$ ☐

$7.3 + 4.1 =$ ☐ $7.9 + 2.2 =$ ☐

$5.6 + 12.8 =$ ☐ $1.2 + 3.9 =$ ☐

$3.8 + 4.21 =$ ☐ $3.45 + 0.45 =$ ☐

$12.5 + 6.5 =$ ☐ $4.65 + 0.25 =$ ☐

$8.22 + 7.33 =$ ☐ $2.065 + 0.023 =$ ☐

$1.2 + 3.4 + 2.6 =$ ☐ $5.6 + 2.3 + 5.3 =$ ☐

$6.3 + 0.5 + 4.3 =$ ☐ $7.5 + 4.5 + 3.5 =$ ☐

$7.1 + 8.2 + 9.3 =$ ☐ $7.0 + 6.72 + 2.45 =$ ☐

4) Cressida ran 2.50 mi on Monday, 7.01 mi on Wednesday, and 3.09 mi on Saturday. What is the total distance she ran during this week?

Decimals, Fractions, and Percentages

Percentages are just fractions of 100. For example, 50% is equal to $\frac{50}{100}$, or $\frac{1}{2}$.

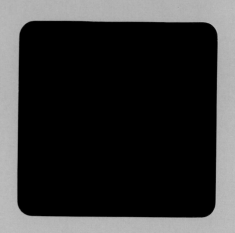

① What is 25% of each number?

8.4 [ ]   12.0 [ ]   6.4 [ ]   20.4 [ ]

6.0 [ ]   9.2 [ ]   16.8 [ ]   440.0 [ ]

② What is 50% of each number?

3.0 [ ]   7.0 [ ]   1.2 [ ]   0.5 [ ]

11.0 [ ]   17.0 [ ]   21.0 [ ]   35.0 [ ]

③ What is 75% of each number?

12.0 [ ]   8.0 [ ]   6.0 [ ]   24.0 [ ]

36.0 [ ]   16.0 [ ]   22.0 [ ]   14.0 [ ]

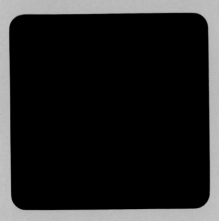

Time Filler:
Do you know how much you weigh to the nearest pound? Step on an electronic scale and find out. Then figure out 50%, 0.25, 10%, and 0.4 of your weight.

(4) Write the answers.

How many minutes is 25% of 1 hour?

What weight is 45% of 10 oz?

How many feet is seven-tenths ($\frac{7}{10}$) of 12.5 ft?

How many kilometers is 30% of 6 km?

How much is 75% of $12?

How many miles is 65% of 200 mi?

How much is 30% more than $5? $5

How many kilometers is 15% more than 2 km?

Decrease 60 yd by 20%.

Decrease $300 by 15%.

Subtraction 1

Are you ready to take away?
Subtraction is the opposite of addition.

① Write the answers.

8.0 − 0.5 = [   ]   9.9 − 7.5 = [   ]

4.0 − 0.3 = [   ]   3.0 − 0.2 = [   ]

5.6 − 2.1 = [   ]   7.0 − 0.9 = [   ]

6.2 − 1.1 = [   ]   7.8 − 5.3 = [   ]

9.4 − 3.4 = [   ]   9.5 − 3.2 = [   ]

9.4 − 6.4 = [   ]   7.8 − 5.6 = [   ]

15.6 − 9.2 = [   ]   12.4 − 7.2 = [   ]

10.2 − 8.7 = [   ]   13.8 − 7.9 = [   ]

14.5 − 8.3 = [   ]   10.6 − 3.5 = [   ]

12.8 − 0.9 = [   ]   16.5 − 12.7 = [   ]

28.9 − 26.3 = [   ]   18.6 − 13.4 = [   ]

29.3 − 17.5 = [   ]   24.7 − 11.9 = [   ]

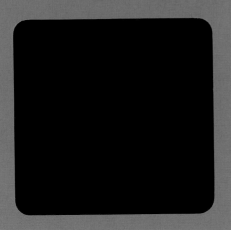

(2) Michael is 55.5 in tall and Marc is 53.7 in tall. What is the difference in their heights?

(3) Solve these subtraction problems.

8.0 − 4.6	6.7 − 3.9	4.3 − 2.8	9.6 − 4.2	5.8 − 1.4
6.43 − 3.29	9.28 − 4.35	6.06 − 2.84	3.0 − 0.8	12.0 − 9.4
8.341 − 2.634	5.078 − 2.563	9.06 − 1.99	4.5 − 3.7	7.0 − 2.9
16.70 − 8.45	14.99 − 11.22	24.62 − 17.54	41.07 − 8.41	12.41 − 8.53

Subtraction 2

Now try some harder subtraction problems. Don't forget to add the symbols for units and money to your answers on page 39.

① Write the answers.

5.347 − 3.200	8.231 − 7.003	7.453 − 4.560	2.951 − 1.460	6.523 − 0.692

12.949 − 4.480	78.623 − 29.860	52.070 − 14.000	27.511 − 13.700	69.653 − 5.170

23.000 − 7.260	85.000 − 43.410	42.000 − 18.244	78.000 − 42.568	35.000 − 17.622

34.060 − 18.040	49.768 − 26.769	23.453 − 15.564	55.172 − 38.081	18.643 − 11.931

10.000 − 4.560	20.000 − 17.641	30.000 − 20.888	40.000 − 27.135	60.000 − 34.259

Time Filler:
Try this extra tricky decimal question. Which answer is the greater decimal number, 44.362 minus 27.731 or 33.767 minus 17.137?

(2) Answer these questions.

Decrease 4.7 cm by 3.8 cm.

What is $12 minus $3.48?

(3) Decrease each length by 0.36 m.

5 m	4.8 m	3.1 m

(4) A path was 7.82 ft long. 1.45 ft of it was grassed over. What is the length of the path now?

(5) Billy had $42.70 but he spent $6.50. How much money does Billy have now?

(6) Middle Brook Street was 5.85 yd wide. A new brick wall reduced the width by 0.68 yd. How wide is the street now?

(7) Sandy has $10.00. She gives $0.75 of it to charity. How much money does Sandy have left?

Beat the Clock 2

Work steadily through these questions.
Do not rush, or you'll make mistakes.
Stay calm and go!

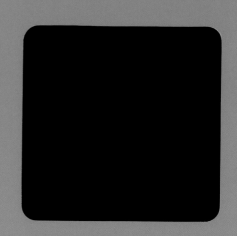

Solve each equation and write the answer.

(1) 5.7 + 3.4 = ☐ (2) 3.8 + 2.1 = ☐ (3) 6.1 + 4.5 = ☐

(4) 7.6 + 5.3 = ☐ (5) 6.4 + 3.6 = ☐ (6) 7.1 + 1.9 = ☐

(7) 5.5 + 3.5 = ☐ (8) 7.2 + 0.8 = ☐ (9) 5.6 + 5.6 = ☐

(10) 7.3 + 6.8 = ☐ (11) 2.9 + 4.6 = ☐ (12) 3.8 + 2.8 = ☐

(13) 2.6 + 3.9 = ☐ (14) 8.0 + 2.9 = ☐ (15) 1.3 + 4.8 = ☐

(16) 0.9 + 0.8 = ☐ (17) 2.3 + 2.8 = ☐ (18) 8.8 + 3.9 = ☐

Solve these slightly harder problems.

(19) 6.34 + 1.06 = ☐ (20) 7.06 + 3.4 = ☐

(21) 0.65 + 0.35 = ☐ (22) 2.06 + 1.04 = ☐

(23) 3.33 + 4.44 = ☐ (24) 4.59 + 6.02 = ☐

(25) 8.05 + 4.89 = ☐ (26) 7.77 + 0.65 = ☐

(27) 1.58 + 7.63 = ☐ (28) 6.63 + 5.09 = ☐

Time Filler:
How did you do? Divide your score by 58 (the number of questions) to give you a decimal amount. Round it to no more than two decimal places. Now figure out your score as a percentage.

Solve these equations.

(29) $5.0 - 0.2 =$ ⬚ (30) $8.0 - 2.3 =$ ⬚ (31) $6.0 - 4.8 =$ ⬚

(32) $12.5 - 3.5 =$ ⬚ (33) $6.4 - 3.2 =$ ⬚ (34) $8.9 - 2.1 =$ ⬚

(35) $10.6 - 3.5 =$ ⬚ (36) $5.1 - 4.0 =$ ⬚ (37) $6.8 - 0.8 =$ ⬚

(38) $20.0 - 6.3 =$ ⬚ (39) $5.3 - 4.2 =$ ⬚ (40) $7.7 - 5.5 =$ ⬚

Find each percentage.

(41) 25% of $5 ⬚ (42) 75% of $16 ⬚ (43) 50% of $9.50 ⬚

(44) 20% of $4 ⬚ (45) 60% of 3 m ⬚ (46) 25% of $0.84 ⬚

(47) 10% of 1.2 m ⬚ (48) 10% of $3.20 ⬚ (49) 65% of $3 ⬚

Write each percentage in its decimal form.

(50) 50% ⬚ (51) 10% ⬚ (52) 70% ⬚

(53) 15% ⬚ (54) 5% ⬚ (55) 45% ⬚

(56) 90% ⬚ (57) 34% ⬚ (58) 1% ⬚

Multiplication 1

When we multiply a decimal by 10, we move the decimal point one place to the right. Can you see what happens when we multiply by 100 and 1,000?

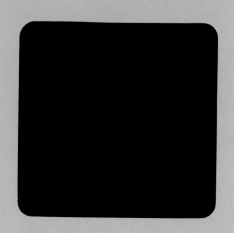

(1) Multiply each number by 10.

5.0 [ ]	7.5 [ ]	8.6 [ ]	0.3 [ ]
4.2 [ ]	0.8 [ ]	7.1 [ ]	5.7 [ ]
7.44 [ ]	9.25 [ ]	3.09 [ ]	5.12 [ ]
3.17 [ ]	0.71 [ ]	8.54 [ ]	0.89 [ ]
2.645 [ ]	7.321 [ ]	76.342 [ ]	41.545 [ ]

(2) Multiply each number by 100.

3.4 [ ]	6.8 [ ]	7.1 [ ]	5.2 [ ]
6.0 [ ]	2.7 [ ]	9.9 [ ]	1.01 [ ]
8.27 [ ]	4.86 [ ]	12.7 [ ]	13.1 [ ]
5.887 [ ]	5.854 [ ]	34.22 [ ]	75.734 [ ]
43.882 [ ]	33.297 [ ]	423.67 [ ]	123.78 [ ]

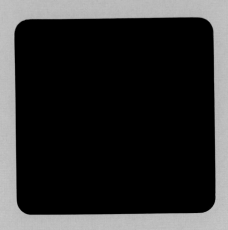

Time Filler:
Here are a few trickier extra questions.
4.4 x 20
8.25 x 300
12.74 x 4,000
When finished, explain how you solved them.

3 Multiply each number by 1,000.

5.6 [ ]   7.1 [ ]   9.6 [ ]   4.0 [ ]

4.3 [ ]   9.2 [ ]   8.1 [ ]   6.8 [ ]

8.3 [ ]   0.001 [ ]   0.07 [ ]   53.999 [ ]

25.19 [ ]   32.132 [ ]   54.67 [ ]   729.7 [ ]

403.2 [ ]   341.56 [ ]   432.11 [ ]   345.678 [ ]

4 Write the answers.

320.006 x 10 [ ]   32.143 x 100 [ ]

29.15 x 1,000 [ ]   201.12 x 10 [ ]

17.487 x 1,000 [ ]   56.195 x 100 [ ]

121.165 x 100 [ ]   782.01 x 1,000 [ ]

812.84 x 100 [ ]   297.49 x 1,000 [ ]

253.786 x 10 [ ]   723.707 x 10 [ ]

Division and Rounding 1

When we divide a decimal number by 10, we move the decimal point one place to the left.

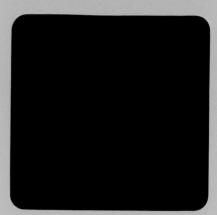

① In what place is 7 in each of these numbers?

2.07	17.63	24.897	315.74
....	....	....	....
7.12	12.37	70.139	29.871
....	....	....	....

② Divide each number by 10.

0.07 [＿＿＿] 80.0 [＿＿＿] 83.86 [＿＿＿] 132.678 [＿＿＿]

24.8 [＿＿＿] 63.96 [＿＿＿] 4.331 [＿＿＿] 87.2 [＿＿＿]

18.4 [＿＿＿] 79.12 [＿＿＿] 5.211 [＿＿＿] 325.986 [＿＿＿]

③ Divide each number by 100.

603.4 [＿＿＿] 720.05 [＿＿＿] 3,300.8 [＿＿＿] 200.005 [＿＿＿]

65.2 [＿＿＿] 7,324.45 [＿＿＿] 723.966 [＿＿＿] 53.06 [＿＿＿]

6.45 [＿＿＿] 7.83 [＿＿＿] 34.32 [＿＿＿] 8.64 [＿＿＿]

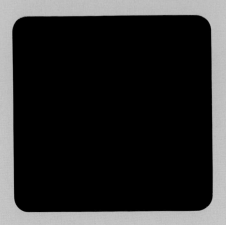

Time Filler:
Write the ages of ten people you know of all different ages. Divide each age by 10 and round to the nearest whole number. These numbers are the approximate number of decades for which each person has been alive.

④ Divide each number by 1,000.

6.3 ⬚   73.85 ⬚   923.357 ⬚   1,854.6 ⬚

0.4 ⬚   18.0 ⬚   75.94 ⬚   50.67 ⬚

⑤ At the zoo, Eliza the Elephant weighs 8,250 lb. Billy the Bear is 0.1 (one-tenth), Chai the Cheetah is 0.01 (one-hundredth), and Polly the Penguin is 0.001 (one-thousandth) of Eliza's weight. How much does each animal weigh?

Chai the Cheetah ⬚   Polly the Penguin ⬚   Billy the Bear ⬚

⑥ Round each of these numbers to the nearest whole number.

66.67 ⬚   3.52 ⬚   253.91 ⬚   504.54 ⬚

25.35 ⬚   4.15 ⬚   621.32 ⬚   698.35 ⬚

48.01 ⬚   3.89 ⬚   481.69 ⬚   523.78 ⬚

Multiplication 2

Multiplication problems can be
written out in horizontal and
vertical forms. Which way do
you prefer?

① Write the answers.

4.2 x 6 = [　　]   2.6 x 8 = [　　]   3.1 x 2 = [　　]

5.9 x 6 = [　　]   9.6 x 8 = [　　]   1.8 x 9 = [　　]

3.8 x 7 = [　　]   6.6 x 4 = [　　]   2.9 x 8 = [　　]

4.7 x 9 = [　　]   5.98 x 5 = [　　]   7.13 x 6 = [　　]

8.15 x 7 = [　　]   3.65 x 4 = [　　]   9.64 x 2 = [　　]

4.56 x 3 = [　　]   8.24 x 2 = [　　]   9.66 x 4 = [　　]

5.69 x 3 = [　　]   8.64 x 7 = [　　]   7.04 x 5 = [　　]

3.08 x 9 = [　　]   7.68 x 6 = [　　]   8.98 x 9 = [　　]

0.65 x 5 = [　　]   1.06 x 7 = [　　]   6.74 x 7 = [　　]

9.81 x 7 = [　　]   8.07 x 8 = [　　]   9.36 x 4 = [　　]

8.05 x 3 = [　　]   1.09 x 6 = [　　]   9.99 x 5 = [　　]

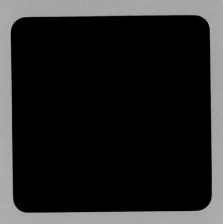

Time Filler:
Make up ten more equations in which decimal numbers are multiplied by whole numbers. Challenge your friends or family to see who can solve them the fastest.

2) Solve these multiplication problems.

6.23	7.98	8.56	2.66
x 12	x 18	x 24	x 31

4.07	3.82	9.27	6.07
x 52	x 68	x 42	x 64

9.99	5.08	1.92	4.15
x 85	x 59	x 13	x 16

7.19	1.39	2.81	7.75
x 19	x 14	x 37	x 45

3) Simone gets $3.55 as allowance every week. Charlie gets $16.50 each month. Who gets the most in a year?

Division

You'll be excellent at dividing decimal numbers when you've worked through these problems. Are you ready? Go!

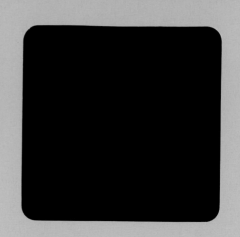

(1) Write the answers.

6.4 ÷ 8 = [ ]   9.6 ÷ 8 = [ ]   7.2 ÷ 9 = [ ]

0.4 ÷ 4 = [ ]   1.7 ÷ 10 = [ ]   0.3 ÷ 10 = [ ]

4.9 ÷ 7 = [ ]   0.36 ÷ 2 = [ ]   0.72 ÷ 12 = [ ]

4.2 ÷ 10 = [ ]   0.48 ÷ 6 = [ ]   0.36 ÷ 4 = [ ]

0.75 ÷ 5 = [ ]   1.08 ÷ 9 = [ ]   1.21 ÷ 11 = [ ]

0.54 ÷ 6 = [ ]   7.28 ÷ 8 = [ ]   8.19 ÷ 9 = [ ]

4.97 ÷ 7 = [ ]   2.46 ÷ 6 = [ ]   4.84 ÷ 4 = [ ]

(2) Emily, Tom, and Sky have a yard sale and make $152.25. The money is divided equally between five charities. How much does each charity receive?

[ ]

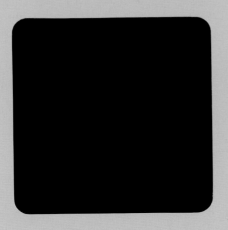

Time Filler:
Try these two extra questions. Katya has $16.92 and wants to divide it equally between four friends. How much does each friend get? She also has 1.32 l of juice and wants to pour it into three glasses in equal amounts. How much juice should each glass have?

3 Write the answers.

$4.32 \div 9 = \boxed{}$ $13.8 \div 6 = \boxed{}$ $27.3 \div 7 = \boxed{}$

$16.3 \div 5 = \boxed{}$ $32.8 \div 4 = \boxed{}$ $77.4 \div 9 = \boxed{}$

$64.6 \div 8 = \boxed{}$ $48.1 \div 5 = \boxed{}$ $81.9 \div 9 = \boxed{}$

$87.5 \div 7 = \boxed{}$ $29.7 \div 4 = \boxed{}$ $46.8 \div 4 = \boxed{}$

$89.7 \div 3 = \boxed{}$ $93.5 \div 2 = \boxed{}$ $69.3 \div 3 = \boxed{}$

$88.4 \div 4 = \boxed{}$ $12.99 \div 6 = \boxed{}$ $16.56 \div 8 = \boxed{}$

$28.15 \div 5 = \boxed{}$ $22.76 \div 4 = \boxed{}$ $39.12 \div 3 = \boxed{}$

$53.92 \div 8 = \boxed{}$ $63.27 \div 9 = \boxed{}$ $61.12 \div 8 = \boxed{}$

$53.12 \div 8 = \boxed{}$ $76.44 \div 6 = \boxed{}$ $72.36 \div 4 = \boxed{}$

$75.45 \div 5 = \boxed{}$ $72.24 \div 6 = \boxed{}$ $60.41 \div 10 = \boxed{}$

$80.15 \div 7 = \boxed{}$ $102.2 \div 7 = \boxed{}$ $104.8 \div 2 = \boxed{}$

Division and Rounding 2

After you've solved these problems, you can check your answers with a calculator.

1 Solve each problem. Round the answer to the nearest penny.

$7 ÷ 3

$15 ÷ 7

$31 ÷ 5

$47 ÷ 3

$18.50 ÷ 3

$2.43 ÷ 6

$7.42 ÷ 9

$7.32 ÷ 4

$0.75 ÷ 4

$1.50 ÷ 7

$3 ÷ 9

$2.99 ÷ 4

2 Solve each problem. Round the answer to the nearest centimeter.
(**Hint:** 100 cm = 1 m)

9 m ÷ 7

16 m ÷ 6

45 m ÷ 4

69 m ÷ 2

7 m ÷ 3

26 m ÷ 4

69 m ÷ 5

72 m ÷ 7

3.6 m ÷ 5

4.28 m ÷ 3

12.65 m ÷ 6

7.4 m ÷ 3

12.9 m ÷ 8

8.12 m ÷ 5

18.8 m ÷ 6

25.6 m ÷ 7

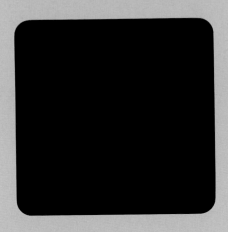

Time Filler:
Find a recipe for a cake in a book. Imagine that you need just half the amount of each ingredient. Figure out the new amounts of flour, sugar, etc. Now imagine you need just one-third of the original amounts. Again, figure out the quantities you now need.

③ Solve each problem. Round the answer to the nearest gram.
(**Hint:** 1,000 g = 1 kg)

4 kg ÷ 6	19 kg ÷ 9	23 kg ÷ 12	12 kg ÷ 7

4.7 kg ÷ 6	11.9 kg ÷ 9	18.4 kg ÷ 7	16.9 kg ÷ 3

④ Solve each problem. Round the answer to the nearest meter.
(**Hint:** 1,000 m = 1 km)

2 km ÷ 3	17 km ÷ 8	38 km ÷ 6	33 km ÷ 5

1.78 km ÷ 4	2.06 km ÷ 9	3.63 km ÷ 5	20.4 km ÷ 7

⑤ Solve each problem. Round the answer to the nearest milliliter.
(**Hint:** 1,000 ml = 1 l)

8 l ÷ 6	13 l ÷ 4	40 l ÷ 7	46 l ÷ 8

23 l ÷ 9	43 l ÷ 5	62 l ÷ 3	17 l ÷ 8

Division and Rounding 3

You can use a calculator to check your answers here. Don't forget to add symbols for units and money.

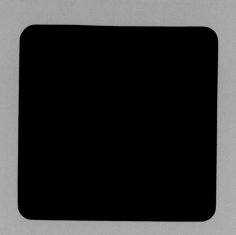

---

① Figure out each answer and round to the nearest dollar.

$17.89 ÷ 3

$26.50 ÷ 4

$30 ÷ 7

$37.15 ÷ 6

$275 ÷ 3

$723 ÷ 6

$26 ÷ 6

$295 ÷ 4

---

② Solve each division problem. Round the answer to the nearest meter.

34.8 m ÷ 7

41.9 m ÷ 7

60.34 m ÷ 4

28.4 m ÷ 3

2,364 m ÷ 7

406 m ÷ 14

3,186 m ÷ 12

5,123 m ÷ 11

③ Solve each problem and round the answer to the nearest inch.

253 in ÷ 7

412 in ÷ 7

372 in ÷ 5

789 in ÷ 7

89 in ÷ 3

142 in ÷ 7

56.86 in ÷ 4

14.19 in ÷ 5

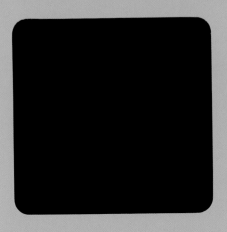

Time Filler:
Make up ten of your own division problems using units of money, weight, volume, and length. Solve them yourself, and then test them on a friend or one of your family members.

(4) Solve each problem and round to the nearest gram.

43 g ÷ 2   317 g ÷ 6   500 g ÷ 6

534 g ÷ 7   250 g ÷ 9   890 g ÷ 12

(5) Do each division problem and round to the nearest penny.

$2 ÷ 3 $53.60 ÷ 7 $120 ÷ 11 $28.30 ÷ 9

$85.62 ÷ 4 $49.12 ÷ 6 $59.52 ÷ 3 $72.12 ÷ 8

(6) Solve each division problem and round to the nearest liter.

582 l ÷ 5   20.16 l ÷ 3   324 l ÷ 6   429 l ÷ 7

456 l ÷ 5   63.85 l ÷ 3   10.02 l ÷ 6   256 l ÷ 7

Decimals and Percentages 1

Remember, all percentages have a decimal equivalent. For example, 75% is the same as 0.75.

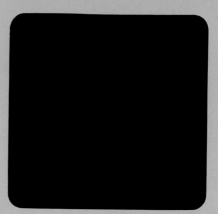

1 What is 70% of each amount?

$6

$23

6.5 ft

37 ft

2 Write each decimal as its percentage equivalent.

0.75

0.45

0.333

0.125

0.01

0.9

0.375

0.3

3 Write each percentage in its decimal form.

55%

25%

12.5%

5%

65%

40%

80%

95%

4 What is 35% of each amount?

6 ft

4 mi

$12

7 ft

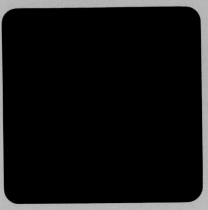

Time Filler:
Here's an extra question: Which amount of money is bigger, 15% of $5 or 90% of $0.80?

---

(5) What is 5% of each amount?

$16	200 ft	$4.60	60 ft

---

(6) What percentage of 200 is each of the following?

50	10	75	150

---

(7) What percentage of 500 cm is each of the following?

50 cm	20 cm	25 cm	2 m

---

(8) What percentage of $5 is each of the following?

$1	$3	$4.50	$0.10

---

(9) What percentage of 150 is each of the following?

30	15	45	90

Decimals and Percentages 2

Make sure you read each question very carefully, so you know exactly how to solve it. Are you ready?

1. A highway was originally 40 mi long but has had its length increased to 60 mi. By what percentage has the highway increased in length?

   ....

2. David usually receives $5 allowance per week, but on his tenth birthday, his parents raised the amount by 10%. How much weekly allowance will David receive now?

   ....

3. Sean measured himself on his ninth birthday and was 45 in tall. On his tenth birthday he measured himself again, and this time he was 54 in tall. By what percentage has Sean grown?

   ....

4. A container carries 2,000 new TVs. When it is opened, 5% of the TVs are found to be broken. How many TVs are not broken?

   .... TVs

5. Emmie usually spends $80 a week on food shopping. Before the holidays, she increased this amount by 25%. How much money will Emmie spend per week now?

   ....

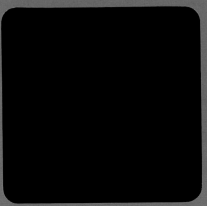

6. Victoria sends 500 texts per month. While on vacation, this number decreases by 70%. How many texts does Victoria send while on vacation?

☐ texts

7. A television show lasts for one hour, but 0.125 of this time is taken up by commercials. How long is the show without the commercials?

☐

8. What percentage of $1,000 is $50?

☐

9. The area of a soccer field in a stadium is 8,000 m². After alterations, the area is reduced by 15%. What is the new area of the field?

☐

10. An amount of money is increased by 35% and is now $27. How much was the amount before the increase?

☐

Estimation and Rounding

Rounding and estimation are useful tools. Practice your skills here.

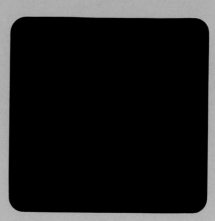

(1) Round each amount to the nearest 10 dollars.

$12,753	$27,056	$70,000.24	$38,005.18

(2) Round each amount to the nearest 100 dollars.

$51	$62,348	$92,062	$72,858

(3) Estimate the answers.

10.18 x 12	42.7 x 15	0.23 x 49	37.1 x 18

1.66 x 6	4.94 x 9	56 x 0.8	7.9 x 12

650 x 0.6	412 x 0.8	1,329 x 0.2	2,153 x 0.5

6.82 x 7	2.19 x 8	37 x 0.9	56 x 1.8

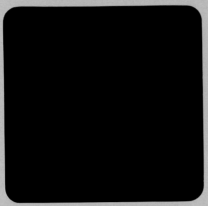

Time Filler:
Why do we have different units of length and weight? Why is it is easier to measure the length of small things in inches, rather than in feet, yards, or miles? Why is it easier to use ounces or grams to weigh ingredients in a recipe, rather than pounds or kilograms?

(4) Round each amount to nearest kilogram.

12,481 g　　　26,099 g　　　245,034 g　　　45,108 g

(5) Round each distance to the nearest kilometer.

6,783 m　　　15,480 m　　　274,199 m　　　482,715 m

(6) The cost of a cell phone is $480. During a sale, it is sold for $360. By what percentage has the price been reduced?

(7) Copper piping is sold in lengths of 2.35 yd. A plumber needs 15 yd of piping. How many lengths will he need?

_____ lengths

(8) Gas at a gas station costs $3.36 per gallon. How many whole gallons will $20 buy?

Solving Problems 1

These problems will test the math skills
you've already covered in this book.
You can solve them!

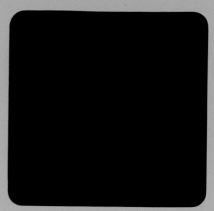

1 Which is larger, 30% of $20 or 15% of $50?

....

What is the difference between the two amounts?

2 Which is longer, 20% of 180 m or 45% of 400 m?

....

What is the difference between the two lengths?

3 Which weighs more, 18% of 3 lb or 12% of 4 lb?

....

What is the difference between the weights?

4 In minutes and seconds, how much
is 12.5% of 1 hour?

....

5 A plane trip is 7.5 hours long. If 80% of the trip
has already passed, how much more time will
it take to complete the trip?

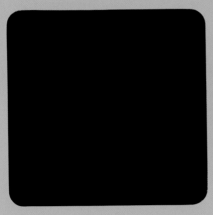

Time Filler:
Are you ready for another problem? Scott made a pie and divided it into nine equal slices. Lizzie ate two slices and Craig ate five! What percentage of the cake did Lizzie eat and what percentage did Craig eat? Round your answers to the nearest percent.

---

6) Divide 6% of 300 by 0.4 of 30.

---

7) Susan gives 10% of her salary to charity each month. If Susan is paid $1,780 each month, how much will she give to charity each year?

$100

$100

---

8) What amount is...

... 15% less than $500?

... 45% more than $5,000?

9) What percentage of...

... 84 is 21?

... 400 is 20?

---

10) Fill in the boxes.

Reduce 4 mi by 2%.

Increase 6 lb by 3.5%.

Solving Problems 2

Read each question slowly and think carefully. Rushing will increase the risk of making mistakes.

(1) What number is 60% more than each of these?

180

340

750

(2) What is 0.01 of each amount? Write your answers in dollars.

$12

$250

$800

(3) When a number is multiplied by 1.78, the result is 21.36. What is the number?

(4) Solve these riddles.

40% of a number is 12. What is the number?

36% of a number is 72. What is the number?

70% of a number is 98. What is the number?

0.7 of a number is 14. What is the number?

0.3 of a number is 5.4. What is the number?

0.2 of a number is 2. What is the number?

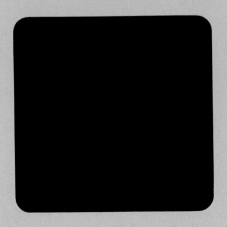

Time Filler:
Try this extra problem: Grandma Jones gives her three grandchildren $8 to share. Charlie, the oldest, takes 45% of the money. Joanna, in the middle, takes 35%. Alexander, the youngest, is left with 20%. How much money does each receive?

5 If a van travels at an average speed of 34.8 mph, how far will it travel in 5 hours?

....

6 Figure out the answers.

If 64 is 0.8 of a number, what is the number?

What is 0.72 of 119?

If 35 is 0.5 of a number, what is the number?

What is 0.29 of 520?

7 Nola usually scores 80 out of 100 on math tests. After studying very hard, her score goes up by 15%. What is Nola's score now?

....

8 At the beginning of the year, a gold coin cost $450. By the end of the year, its cost went up by 25%. What is its cost at the end of the year?

$100

....

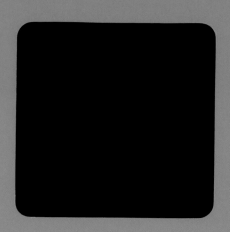

Beat the Clock 3

Do your very best! If you're not happy with your score or time, try this quick-fire round again tomorrow to see if you can improve.

Multiply each number by 10.

(1) 7.5 [ ]   (2) 16.8 [ ]   (3) 0.03 [ ]

Multiply each number by 100.

(4) 7.09 [ ]   (5) 24.05 [ ]   (6) 3.06 [ ]

Multiply each number by 1,000.

(7) 0.5 [ ]   (8) 3.88 [ ]   (9) 100.1 [ ]

Divide each number by 10.

(10) 4.6 [ ]   (11) 60.1 [ ]   (12) 103.0 [ ]

Divide each number by 100.

(13) 16.0 [ ]   (14) 4,250 [ ]   (15) 30.05 [ ]

Divide each number by 1,000.

(16) 43,967 [ ]   (17) 132,900 [ ]   (18) 78,519 [ ]

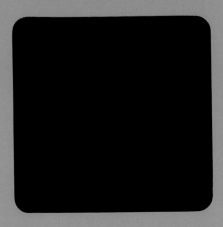

Time Filler:
Now you're a decimal-numbers expert! If you want more practice, write your own mini "Beat the clock" page, with a mixture of 20 addition, subtraction, multiplication, and division problems.

Round each number to two decimal places.

(19) 4.893 [　　] (20) 6.888 [　　] (21) 8.005 [　　]

(22) 17.006 [　　] (23) 31.416 [　　] (24) 24.435 [　　]

(25) 65.007 [　　] (26) 80.005 [　　] (27) 236.991 [　　]

Round each number to three decimal places.

(28) 2.8745 [　　] (29) 0.5555 [　　] (30) 1.0007 [　　]

(31) 52.0502 [　　] (32) 6.3512 [　　] (33) 28.6891 [　　]

Quickly write the answers.

(34) 2 x 0.6 [　　] (35) 12 x 1.2 [　　] (36) 16 x 0.3 [　　]

(37) 2.7 x 5 [　　] (38) 0.2 x 75 [　　] (39) 0.6 x 500 [　　]

(40) 3.8 x 4 [　　] (41) 2.8 x 0.5 [　　] (42) 0.3 x 0.3 [　　]

(43) 24 x 0.25 [　　] (44) 0.7 x 0.4 [　　] (45) 30% of 60 [　　]

(46) 25% of 1 [　　] (47) 45% of 400 [　　] (48) 300 x 0.75 [　　]

Answers:

04–05 Equivalents 1
06–07 Equivalents 2

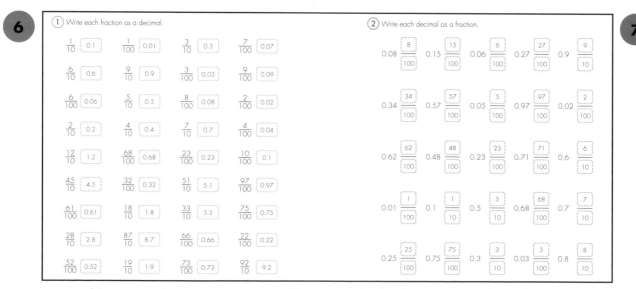

4

1. Shade in 0.5 of each shape.

2. Shade in 0.25 of each shape.

3. Shade in 0.75 of each shape.

4. Write each decimal as a fraction.

$0.5 \frac{1}{2}$ $0.25 \frac{1}{4}$ $0.75 \frac{3}{4}$

5. Draw lines linking each decimal amount to the shape with the equivalent area shaded.

0.5

0.25

0.75

5

6. What decimal amount of each shape has been shaded?

0.75   0.25

0.5   0.5

0.25   0.5

0.5   0.5

7. Write the corresponding decimal for each shaded portion.

0.5

0.75

Your child should quickly recognize how much of each shape is shaded, including more complex shapes or places where six out of eight parts are shaded. He or she should easily translate $\frac{6}{8}$ to $\frac{3}{4}$, for example, and then to 0.75 without being reminded.

6

1. Write each fraction as a decimal.

$\frac{1}{10}$ 0.1 $\frac{1}{100}$ 0.01 $\frac{3}{10}$ 0.3 $\frac{7}{100}$ 0.07

$\frac{6}{10}$ 0.6 $\frac{9}{10}$ 0.9 $\frac{3}{100}$ 0.03 $\frac{9}{100}$ 0.09

$\frac{6}{100}$ 0.06 $\frac{5}{10}$ 0.5 $\frac{8}{100}$ 0.08 $\frac{2}{100}$ 0.02

$\frac{2}{10}$ 0.2 $\frac{4}{10}$ 0.4 $\frac{7}{10}$ 0.7 $\frac{4}{100}$ 0.04

$\frac{12}{10}$ 1.2 $\frac{68}{100}$ 0.68 $\frac{23}{100}$ 0.23 $\frac{10}{100}$ 0.1

$\frac{45}{10}$ 4.5 $\frac{32}{100}$ 0.32 $\frac{51}{10}$ 5.1 $\frac{97}{100}$ 0.97

$\frac{61}{100}$ 0.61 $\frac{18}{10}$ 1.8 $\frac{33}{10}$ 3.3 $\frac{75}{100}$ 0.75

$\frac{28}{10}$ 2.8 $\frac{87}{10}$ 8.7 $\frac{66}{100}$ 0.66 $\frac{22}{100}$ 0.22

$\frac{52}{100}$ 0.52 $\frac{19}{10}$ 1.9 $\frac{73}{100}$ 0.73 $\frac{92}{10}$ 9.2

7

2. Write each decimal as a fraction.

$0.08 \frac{8}{100}$ $0.15 \frac{15}{100}$ $0.06 \frac{6}{100}$ $0.27 \frac{27}{100}$ $0.9 \frac{9}{10}$

$0.34 \frac{34}{100}$ $0.57 \frac{57}{100}$ $0.05 \frac{5}{100}$ $0.97 \frac{97}{100}$ $0.02 \frac{2}{100}$

$0.62 \frac{62}{100}$ $0.48 \frac{48}{100}$ $0.23 \frac{23}{100}$ $0.71 \frac{71}{100}$ $0.6 \frac{6}{10}$

$0.01 \frac{1}{100}$ $0.1 \frac{1}{10}$ $0.5 \frac{5}{10}$ $0.68 \frac{68}{100}$ $0.7 \frac{7}{10}$

$0.25 \frac{25}{100}$ $0.75 \frac{75}{100}$ $0.3 \frac{3}{10}$ $0.03 \frac{3}{100}$ $0.8 \frac{8}{10}$

In some of the answers, it may be possible to simplify the solution. For example, $\frac{5}{10}$ can be simplified to $\frac{1}{2}$. Your child will be learning to simplify fractions at school at the same time as this work, so expect some of these answers to be in a simplified form.

Answers:

08–09 Dividing by 10 and 100

10–11 Rounding Decimals

8

① Write whether 1 is in the tens, ones, tenths, or hundredths place.

1.0	0.1	0.01	2.1	32.01
Ones	Tenths	Hundredths	Tenths	Hundredths

4.12	21.8	7.1	1.2	10.6
Tenths	Ones	Tenths	Ones	Tens

② Suki has a total of $13.68 in her piggy bank. Which part of that number is the ones place and which is the tenths place?

Ones 3

Tenths 6

③ Divide each number by 10 and write the answer in the decimal form.

50	5.0	4	0.4	81	8.1	70	7.0	25	2.5
7	0.7	35	3.5	60	6.0	90	9.0	5	0.5
15	1.5	11	1.1	18	1.8	20	2.0	32	3.2

9

④ Divide each number by 100 and write the answer in the decimal form.

78	0.78	12	0.12	43	0.43	9	0.09	99	0.99
40	0.4	5	0.05	66	0.66	1	0.01	50	0.5
32	0.32	10	0.1	70	0.7	55	0.55	92	0.92

⑤ Write whether 5 is in the tens, ones, tenths, or hundredths place.

56.3	7.05	0.5	5.62	0.05
Tens	Hundredths	Tenths	Ones	Hundredths

15.2	12.5	51.9	20.5	5.78
Ones	Tenths	Tens	Tenths	Ones

⑥ Write whether 8 is in the tens, ones, tenths, or hundredths place.

7.68	8.6	9.83	12.08	8.43
Hundredths	Ones	Tenths	Hundredths	Ones

4.81	10.8	8.24	6.38	18.5
Tenths	Tenths	Ones	Hundredths	Ones

When solving 40 divided by 10, for example, it is not strictly necessary to write the answer as 4.0. An answer of 4 would also be correct. However, it can be helpful to write the full form so your child becomes used to thinking in the decimal format.

10

① Round each decimal to the nearest whole number.

6.3	6	7.6	8	9.8	10
4.2	4	0.5	1	24.5	25
24.9	25	15.5	16	15.7	16
42.5	43	12.1	12	49.8	50
18.2	18	56.4	56	79.5	80
17.3	17	89.5	90	57.7	58
93.9	94	69.9	70	87.9	88
88.4	88	88.5	89	88.6	89
68.5	69	85.6	86	65.8	66
32.7	33	73.3	73	88.8	89
90.5	91	42.6	43	59.1	59
40.5	41	52.5	53	73.4	73

11

② Round each decimal to the nearest whole unit.

4.5 in	5 in	3.8 m	4 m	7.1 km	7 km
56.4 g	56 g	2.3 mi	2 mi	12.5 g	13 g
66.6 m	67 m	86.5 ft	87 ft	42.8 lb	43 lb
47.6 ft	48 ft	17.3 cm	17 cm	19.1 km	19 km
15.5 cm	16 cm	81.7 mm	82 mm	23.7 kg	24 kg
14.2 g	14 g	56.5 m	57 m	68.8 mi	69 mi
49.2 ft	49 ft	35.7 in	36 in	26.6 mm	27 mm
76.4 m	76 m	76.5 cm	77 cm	76.6 ft	77 ft
67.5 g	68 g	57.2 lb	57 lb	57.7 km	58 km

③ Caleb's favorite book is 8.2 in wide, 10.5 in long, and 0.7 in thick. Round these measurements to the nearest inch.

8 in   11 in   1 in

The main stumbling block here is the "halfway" point of 5 where some children are unsure about rounding up or down. Remind them that the standard rule is to always go upward from 5; for example, 76.5 would become 77.

Answers:

12–13 Comparing Decimals 1
14–15 Measurements and Money

---

12 · **13**

① Circle the larger number in each pair.

3.6 (6.3)	4.8 (8.4)	3.5 (3.8)	(9.0) 8.9
(5.3) 4.9	(8.0) 6.9	12.3 (13.3)	23.3 (33.2)
21.2 (22.1)	35.8 (58.3)	(18.6) 16.8	31.5 (35.1)
2.9 (9.2)	1.5 (2.5)	(19.8) 18.9	(34.1) 33.9
80.1 (80.9)	(26.3) 23.6	14.7 (17.4)	(55.4) 54.5

② Circle the smallest number in each group.

23.2 (22.3) 23.3   48.7 (47.8) 48.8   54.6 56.4 (54.5)

③ Circle the largest number in each group.

(28.3) 23.8 28.2   (95.5) 59.5 55.9   63.4 (64.3) 63.2

④ Circle the smaller amount in each pair.

(24.6 mm) 26.4 mm	($2.58) $2.85	(17.9 ft) 19.7 ft
(5.48 in) 5.84 in	17.25 cm (12.75 cm)	(24.82 g) 28.42 g
(0.67 g) 0.76 g	(1.89 in) 1.98 in	3.83 oz (3.38 oz)
(29.4 cm) 49.2 cm	34.3 mi (33.4 mi)	(97.8 g) 98.7 g
(2.41 oz) 4.21 oz	(0.58 in) 1.29 in	(9.09 g) 9.13 g

⑤ Circle the larger amount in each pair.

8.09 g (8.9 g)   (8.8 in) 0.65 in   0.56 cm (1.01 cm)

⑥ Circle the smallest amount in each group.

18.06 mi (18.04 mi) 18.1 mi   36.67 kg 37.67 kg (36.66 kg)

Remind your child to pay special attention to what is being asked for—larger or smaller. This tests knowledge of place value. Your child should organize the numbers by looking at the tens column first, followed by the ones, tenths, and hundredths, and then comparing their values.

---

14 · **15**

① Alex runs 1.82 mi, Mike runs 1.28 mi, and Harris runs 1.56 mi. Who runs farther than Harris?

Alex

② Answer these questions.

How much longer is 1.45 m than 1.35 m?   0.1 m

Which weighs more, 2.56 kg or 2.65 kg?   2.65 kg

Which of these measurements is the same as 108 cm?

10.8 m   1.8 m   1.08 m   1.08 m

③ Clara has 0.4 lb of fruit; Katie has double that amount. How much fruit does Katie have?   0.8 lb

David has half Clara's amount. How much fruit does David have?   0.2 lb

④ Rosie believes 186 cm is the same as 1.86 m. Is she correct?   Yes

Olly says 190 cm is 10 cm less than 2 m. Is he correct?   Yes

⑤ Write each amount in cents (¢).

$3.50	$2.28	$0.67	$10.40
350 ¢	228 ¢	67 ¢	1,040 ¢
$1.45	$1.54	$4.51	$5.14
145 ¢	154 ¢	451 ¢	514 ¢

⑥ Write each amount as dollars.

467 ¢	273 ¢	95 ¢	608 ¢
$4.67	$2.73	$0.95	$6.08
384 ¢	529 ¢	77 ¢	999 ¢
$3.84	$5.29	$0.77	$9.99

⑦ What is three-quarters ($\frac{3}{4}$) of each amount? Give your answers in dollars.

| $4 | $1 | $10 | $8 |
| $3 | $0.75 | $7.50 | $6 |

⑧ Gary's pencil is 4.98 in long, Larry's pencil is 4.94 in long, and Harry's pencil is 4.96 in long. Who has the shortest pencil?

Larry

The key to these problems is figuring out what operation is needed. Once that is established, the solution should be straightforward. The more practice your child has with simple "real-life" problems, the better.

Answers:

16–17 Equivalents 3

18–19 Equivalents 4

20–21 Beat the Clock 1, see p.80

16 / **17**

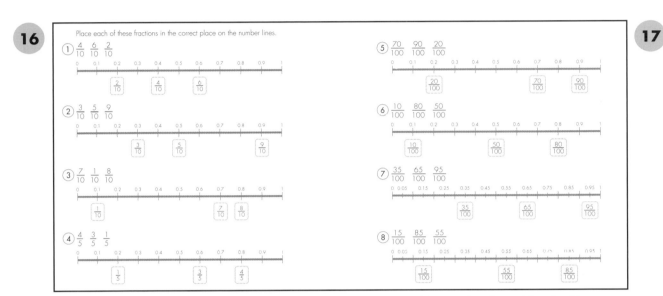

Your child needs to be careful about placing the required fraction on the number line by taking careful note of tenths and hundredths.

18 / **19**

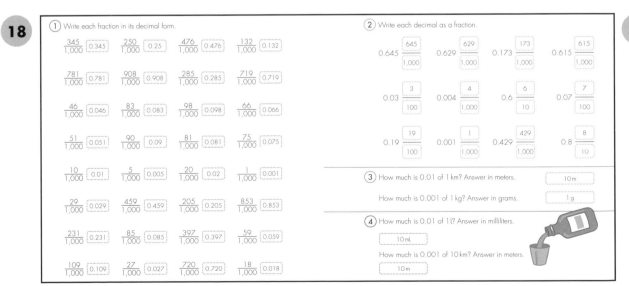

A number such as 0.48 is sometimes shown as just .48 but it is helpful to your child if he or she becomes used to using a fuller format for decimal amounts. Writing out the decimal form of a fraction, and vice versa, may seem tricky at first. So, the more practice, the better.

Answers:

22–23 Addition 1
24–25 Addition 2

22

① Find the totals.

$3 + 1.5 =$ 4.5 $5 + 2.5 =$ 7.5

$8.3 + 4 =$ 12.3 $6.4 + 5 =$ 11.4

$7 + 0.2 =$ 7.2 $1 + 1.4 =$ 2.4

$6.9 + 3 =$ 9.9 $5 + 2.2 =$ 7.2

$7.4 + 3 =$ 10.4 $12.3 + 8 =$ 20.3

$2.4 + 6 =$ 8.4 $4.4 + 6 =$ 10.4

$12 + 8.6 =$ 20.6 $17.4 + 3 =$ 20.4

$18.7 + 6 =$ 24.7 $7.3 + 7 =$ 14.3

$14 + 0.7 =$ 14.7 $24 + 0.3 =$ 24.3

② On vacation, Richard spends 3 days in France, 0.5 days in Luxembourg, 2.5 days in Belgium, and 3.5 days in the Netherlands, then goes home. How long was Richard's trip?

9.5 days

23

③ Find the totals.

$3 + 4.6 + 2 =$ 9.6 $1.2 + 3 + 5 =$ 9.2

$6 + 8 + 3.5 =$ 17.5 $6 + 4 + 0.1 =$ 10.1

$6.3 + 4 + 4 =$ 14.3 $4.5 + 6 + 3 =$ 13.5

$8 + 3.9 + 3 =$ 14.9 $7.9 + 1 + 3 =$ 11.9

$4.6 + 4 + 6 =$ 14.6 $0.9 + 1 + 7 =$ 8.9

$9.1 + 9 + 2 =$ 20.1 $0.6 + 4 + 5 =$ 9.6

$3.4 + 5 + 6 =$ 14.4 $8 + 9 + 5.4 =$ 22.4

$7 + 6.3 + 4 =$ 17.3 $6.6 + 6 + 6 =$ 18.6

$6 + 4.3 + 12 =$ 22.3 $5.1 + 9 + 3 =$ 17.1

$4.8 + 6 + 9 =$ 19.8 $17 + 3 + 0.2 =$ 20.2

$7 + 2.2 + 8 =$ 17.2 $12 + 7 + 5.9 =$ 24.9

$4 + 7 + 6.9 =$ 17.9 $24 + 8 + 0.8 =$ 32.8

With these questions, your child needs to recognize the values of each figure, especially the decimals. Although the addition is fairly easy, remind your child that he or she needs to be careful when the decimal amount appears first—as in 0.4 + 3, for example—which can sometimes be confusing.

24

① Write the answers.

$2.5\,ft + 4\,ft =$ 6.5 ft $5.9\,g + 7\,g =$ 12.9 g

$17\,ft + 2.8\,ft =$ 19.8 ft $7\,ft + 4.3\,ft =$ 11.3 ft

$4.3\,g + 9.4\,g =$ 13.7 g $9.5\,g + 5\,g =$ 14.5 g

$6.2\,g + 4.1\,g =$ 10.3 g $1.8\,kg + 3\,kg =$ 4.8 kg

$7.1\,m + 3.4\,m =$ 10.5 m $6.5\,g + 4.4\,g =$ 10.9 g

$3\,mi + 4.2\,mi =$ 7.2 mi $8\,ft + 3.4\,ft =$ 11.4 ft

$12\,in + 4.8\,in =$ 16.8 in $12.5\,g + 3.4\,g =$ 15.9 g

$6.3\,kg + 9.6\,kg =$ 15.9 kg $8.5\,ml + 6.3\,ml =$ 14.8 ml

$8\,lb + 2.4\,lb =$ 10.4 lb $3.7\,ml + 2.2\,ml =$ 5.9 ml

② Kim and Harry plant some flowers in their garden. They plant 2.75 ft² with roses and 1.75 ft² with daisies. What is the total area they planted with flowers?

4.5 ft²

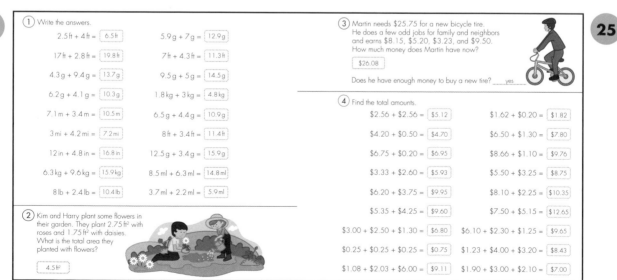

25

③ Martin needs $25.75 for a new bicycle tire. He does a few odd jobs for family and neighbors and earns $8.15, $5.20, $3.23, and $9.50. How much money does Martin have now?

$26.08

Does he have enough money to buy a new tire? ____ yes

④ Find the total amounts.

$\$2.56 + \$2.56 =$ $5.12 $\$1.62 + \$0.20 =$ $1.82

$\$4.20 + \$0.50 =$ $4.70 $\$6.50 + \$1.30 =$ $7.80

$\$6.75 + \$0.20 =$ $6.95 $\$8.66 + \$1.10 =$ $9.76

$\$3.33 + \$2.60 =$ $5.93 $\$5.50 + \$3.25 =$ $8.75

$\$6.20 + \$3.75 =$ $9.95 $\$8.10 + \$2.25 =$ $10.35

$\$5.35 + \$4.25 =$ $9.60 $\$7.50 + \$5.15 =$ $12.65

$\$3.00 + \$2.50 + \$1.30 =$ $6.80 $\$6.10 + \$2.30 + \$1.25 =$ $9.65

$\$0.25 + \$0.25 + \$0.25 =$ $0.75 $\$1.23 + \$4.00 + \$3.20 =$ $8.43

$\$1.08 + \$2.03 + \$6.00 =$ $9.11 $\$1.90 + \$3.00 + \$2.10 =$ $7.00

These questions continue with simple addition, although now units of measure are included. Your child should get into the habit of always writing the units. The final questions on these pages involve some carrying over, a skill your child will have learned in school. Remind your child to be careful when solving these types of problems.

Answers:

26–27 Comparing Decimals 2
28–29 Addition 3

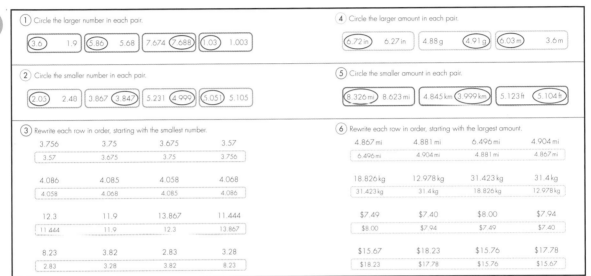

26

① Circle the larger number in each pair.

| (3.6) 1.9 | (5.86) 5.68 | 7.674 (7.688) | (1.03) 1.003 |

② Circle the smaller number in each pair.

| (2.03) 2.48 | 3.867 (3.847) | 5.231 (4.999) | (5.051) 5.105 |

③ Rewrite each row in order, starting with the smallest number.

| 3.756 | 3.75 | 3.675 | 3.57 |
| 3.57 | 3.675 | 3.75 | 3.756 |

| 4.086 | 4.085 | 4.058 | 4.068 |
| 4.058 | 4.068 | 4.085 | 4.086 |

| 12.3 | 11.9 | 13.867 | 11.444 |
| 11.444 | 11.9 | 12.3 | 13.867 |

| 8.23 | 3.82 | 2.83 | 3.28 |
| 2.83 | 3.28 | 3.82 | 8.23 |

27

④ Circle the larger amount in each pair.

| (6.72 in) 6.27 in | 4.88 g (4.91 g) | (6.03 m) 3.6 m |

⑤ Circle the smaller amount in each pair.

| (8.326 mi) 8.623 mi | 4.845 km (3.999 km) | 5.123 ft (5.104 ft) |

⑥ Rewrite each row in order, starting with the largest amount.

| 4.867 mi | 4.881 mi | 6.496 mi | 4.904 mi |
| 6.496 mi | 4.904 mi | 4.881 mi | 4.867 mi |

| 18.826 kg | 12.978 kg | 31.423 kg | 31.4 kg |
| 31.423 kg | 31.4 kg | 18.826 kg | 12.978 kg |

| $7.49 | $7.40 | $8.00 | $7.94 |
| $8.00 | $7.94 | $7.49 | $7.40 |

| $15.67 | $18.23 | $15.76 | $17.78 |
| $18.23 | $17.78 | $15.76 | $15.67 |

This work will test your child's understanding of place value. If your child is having trouble with these pages, remind him or her that when comparing numbers with different amounts of numerals after the decimal point—like 1.2 and 1.84—you can add zeroes after the digits. In this example, your child might like to change 1.2 to 1.20.

28

① Add the numbers.

$3.6 + 2.8 =$ 6.4 $4.4 + 9.3 =$ 13.7 $7.6 + 2.9 =$ 10.5

$6.25 + 4.4 =$ 10.65 $4.4 + 18.3 =$ 22.7 $7.2 + 11.2 =$ 18.4

$3.71 + 8.81 =$ 12.52 $4.55 + 1.25 =$ 5.8 $3.05 + 2.05 =$ 5.1

$8.92 + 4.19 =$ 13.11 $3.85 + 1.05 =$ 4.9 $12.3 + 3.8 =$ 16.1

$6.12 + 2.08 =$ 8.2 $13.7 + 2.4 =$ 16.1 $29.5 + 6.2 =$ 35.7

② Find the totals.

$3.0 + 6.1 + 7.3 =$ 16.4 $7.3 + 2.4 + 1.6 =$ 11.3

$5.4 + 3.2 + 1.0 =$ 9.6 $2.8 + 6.5 + 3.2 =$ 12.5

$6.7 + 3.9 + 4.9 =$ 15.5 $8.2 + 5.0 + 3.8 =$ 17.0

$4.9 + 8.8 + 1.4 =$ 15.1 $6.5 + 4.5 + 3.5 =$ 14.5

$12.2 + 4.4 + 10.0 =$ 26.6 $13.2 + 5.5 + 12.6 =$ 31.3

29

③ Solve these problems.

4.6	5.6	7.1	9.3	6.1
+ 3.4	+ 6.8	+ 3.4	+ 1.4	+ 4.8
8.0	12.4	10.5	10.7	10.9

12.8	11.6	15.3	24.7	64.8
+ 6.7	+ 4.7	+ 2.9	+ 3.3	+ 7.4
19.5	16.3	18.2	28.0	72.2

4.63	5.89	1.07	4.36	8.26
+ 1.27	+ 2.33	+ 2.46	+ 1.44	+ 1.74
5.90	8.22	3.53	5.80	10.00

60.34	31.23	56.12	23.99	33.93
+ 31.47	+ 14.56	+ 21.08	+ 12.01	+ 83.72
91.81	45.79	77.20	36.00	117.65

④ Each morning, Zara and Kyle walk 0.22 mi to the bus stop, travel 2.39 mi on the bus, and then walk 0.16 mi to reach their school. How far is their journey?

2.77 mi

Your child should become familiar with simple addition problems in both horizontal and vertical forms. Some answers are whole numbers—for example, 50. Although writing just the number is acceptable, you may want to ask your child to write a slightly fuller answer—such as 50.0—as he or she practices working with decimals.

Answers:

30–31 Addition 4

32–33 Addition 5

30

① Find the totals.

3.48 + 5.52 = 9.00   1.09 + 0.91 = 2.00

3.0 + 6.464 = 9.464   4.89 + 2.11 = 7.00

6.042 + 1.1 = 7.142   5.109 + 7.9 = 13.009

5.64 + 2.364 = 8.004   2.34 + 4.001 = 6.341

7.25 + 3.593 = 10.843   7.62 + 3.041 = 10.661

② Solve these addition problems.

2.65	1.783	6.20	9.132	2.391
+ 1.46	+ 2.620	+ 3.88	+ 1.410	+ 0.129
4.11	4.403	10.08	10.542	2.520

52.60	81.230	56.902	7.008	4.150
+ 8.23	+ 3.284	+ 6.700	+ 0.830	+ 1.213
60.83	84.514	63.602	7.838	5.363

23.600	0.600	12.850	4.94	6.403
+ 0.123	+ 3.567	+ 9.006	+ 0.70	+ 4.892
23.723	4.167	21.856	5.64	11.295

31

③ Answer these questions.

How much is $3.56 plus $2.99? $6.55

What is 1.56 yd added to 1.86 yd?   3.42 yd

How much is 1.675 mi increased by 0.255 mi?   1.93 mi

What amount is $2.67 more than $12.50? $15.17

④ A kitchen counter is made up of two pieces. One piece is 5.395 ft long and the other 1.746 ft. What will be the length of the whole counter when the two pieces are joined together?

7.141 ft

⑤ What is the total when $2.85 is added to each of these?

$2.69 $5.54 $4.50 $7.35

⑥ Add this group of numbers and write the total.

2.455   7.234   8.167   17.856

Although some addition problems are written in the horizontal format, your child can rewrite the problem in vertical format if he or she prefers. Great care should be taken with all the questions, especially when the numbers have different amounts of decimal figures, as in 2.1 + 32.045.

32

① A car makes three journeys. The first journey is 8.627 mi, the second is 9.348 mi, and the third is 12.450 mi. How far does the car travel in total?

30.425 mi

② Write the answers.

2.423	1.867	0.655	7.291
+ 1.534	+ 2.427	+ 2.809	+ 0.810
3.957	4.294	3.464	8.101

0.836	2.056	7.340	4.980
+ 6.190	+ 1.006	+ 8.455	+ 2.713
7.026	3.062	15.795	7.693

4.006	3.501	2.956	12.535
+ 1.040	+ 0.660	+ 0.300	+ 6.375
5.046	4.161	3.256	18.910

10.044	12.800	6.834	9.471
2.860	0.640	1.423	1.250
+ 8.009	+ 4.235	+ 0.223	+ 3.089
20.913	17.675	8.480	13.810

33

③ Find the totals.

4.6 + 3.4 = 8.0   6.6 + 3.9 = 10.5

7.3 + 4.1 = 11.4   7.9 + 2.2 = 10.1

5.6 + 12.8 = 18.4   1.2 + 3.9 = 5.1

3.8 + 4.21 = 8.01   3.45 + 0.45 = 3.90

12.5 + 6.5 = 19.0   4.65 + 0.25 = 4.90

8.22 + 7.33 = 15.55   2.065 + 0.023 = 2.088

1.2 + 3.4 + 2.6 = 7.2   5.6 + 2.3 + 5.3 = 13.2

6.3 + 0.5 + 4.3 = 11.1   7.5 + 4.5 + 3.5 = 15.5

7.1 + 8.2 + 9.3 = 24.6   7.0 + 6.72 + 2.45 = 16.17

④ Cressida ran 2.50 mi on Monday, 7.01 mi on Wednesday, and 3.09 mi on Saturday. What is the total distance she ran during this week?

12.6 mi

The addition problems are gradually becoming more difficult, and your child will need to take their time on these pages. Through this practice, your child will become familiar with the addition of three numbers rather than two.

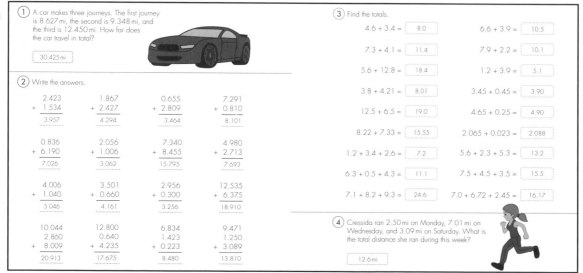

Answers:

34–35 Decimals, Fractions, and Percentages
36–37 Subtraction 1

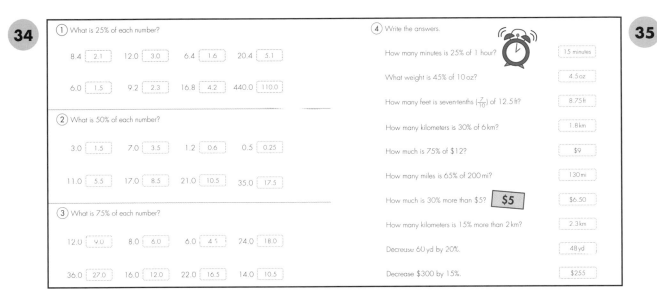

34

① What is 25% of each number?

8.4 [2.1]   12.0 [3.0]   6.4 [1.6]   20.4 [5.1]

6.0 [1.5]   9.2 [2.3]   16.8 [4.2]   440.0 [110.0]

② What is 50% of each number?

3.0 [1.5]   7.0 [3.5]   1.2 [0.6]   0.5 [0.25]

11.0 [5.5]   17.0 [8.5]   21.0 [10.5]   35.0 [17.5]

③ What is 75% of each number?

12.0 [9.0]   8.0 [6.0]   6.0 [4.5]   24.0 [18.0]

36.0 [27.0]   16.0 [12.0]   22.0 [16.5]   14.0 [10.5]

35

④ Write the answers.

How many minutes is 25% of 1 hour?   [15 minutes]

What weight is 45% of 10 oz?   [4.5 oz]

How many feet is seven-tenths ($\frac{7}{10}$) of 12.5 ft?   [8.75 ft]

How many kilometers is 30% of 6 km?   [1.8 km]

How much is 75% of $12?   [$9]

How many miles is 65% of 200 mi?   [130 mi]

How much is 30% more than $5? **$5**   [$6.50]

How many kilometers is 15% more than 2 km?   [2.3 km]

Decrease 60 yd by 20%.   [48 yd]

Decrease $300 by 15%.   [$255]

Your child should have simple conversions between decimal amounts and percentages at his or her fingertips. You may find that he or she is able to solve most of these questions in his or her head.

36

① Write the answers.

8.0 – 0.5 = [7.5]   9.9 – 7.5 = [2.4]

4.0 – 0.3 = [3.7]   3.0 – 0.2 = [2.8]

5.6 – 2.1 = [3.5]   7.0 – 0.9 = [6.1]

6.2 – 1.1 = [5.1]   7.8 – 5.3 = [2.5]

9.4 – 3.4 = [6.0]   9.5 – 3.2 = [6.3]

9.4 – 6.4 = [3.0]   7.8 – 5.6 = [2.2]

15.6 – 9.2 = [6.4]   12.4 – 7.2 = [5.2]

10.2 – 8.7 = [1.5]   13.8 – 7.9 = [5.9]

14.5 – 8.3 = [6.2]   10.6 – 3.5 = [7.1]

12.8 – 0.9 = [11.9]   16.5 – 12.7 = [3.8]

28.9 – 26.3 = [2.6]   18.6 – 13.4 = [5.2]

29.3 – 17.5 = [11.8]   24.7 – 11.9 = [12.8]

37

② Michael is 55.5 in tall and Marc is 53.7 in tall. What is the difference in their heights?

[1.8 in]

③ Solve these subtraction problems.

8.0	6.7	4.3	9.6	5.8
– 4.6	– 3.9	– 2.8	– 4.2	– 1.4
3.4	2.8	1.5	5.4	4.4

6.43	9.28	6.06	3.0	12.0
– 3.29	– 4.35	– 2.84	– 0.8	– 9.4
3.14	4.93	3.22	2.2	2.6

8.341	5.078	9.06	4.5	7.0
– 2.634	– 2.563	– 1.99	– 3.7	– 2.9
5.707	2.515	7.07	0.8	4.1

16.70	14.99	24.62	41.07	12.41
– 8.45	– 11.22	– 17.54	– 8.41	– 8.53
8.25	3.77	7.08	32.66	3.88

If your child prefers vertical subtraction, let him or her rewrite the equations in that format. While solving subtraction problems, be careful to line up numbers in their correct columns.

Answers:

38–39 Subtraction 2

40–41 Beat the Clock 2, see p.80

42–43 Multiplication 1

38

① Write the answers.

5.347	8.231	7.453	2.951	6.523
− 3.200	− 7.003	− 4.560	− 1.460	− 0.692
2.147	1.228	2.893	1.491	5.831

12.949	78.623	52.070	27.511	69.653
− 4.480	− 29.860	− 14.000	− 13.700	− 5.170
8.469	48.763	38.070	13.811	64.483

23.000	85.000	42.000	78.000	35.000
− 7.260	− 43.410	− 18.244	− 42.568	− 17.622
15.740	41.590	23.756	35.432	17.378

34.060	49.768	23.453	55.172	18.643
− 18.040	− 26.769	− 15.564	− 38.081	− 11.931
16.020	22.999	7.889	17.091	6.712

10.000	20.000	30.000	40.000	60.000
− 4.560	− 17.641	− 20.888	− 27.135	− 34.259
5.440	2.359	9.112	12.865	25.741

② Answer these questions.

Decrease 4.7 cm by 3.8 cm. `0.9 cm`

What is $12 minus $3.48? `$8.52`

③ Decrease each length by 0.36 m.

5 m	4.8 m	3.1 m
4.64 m	4.44 m	2.74 m

④ A path was 7.82 ft long. 1.45 ft of it was grassed over. What is the length of the path now?
`6.37 ft`

⑤ Billy had $42.70 but he spent $6.50. How much money does Billy have now? `$36.20`

⑥ Middle Brook Street was 5.85 yd wide. A new brick wall reduced the width by 0.68 yd. How wide is the street now? `5.17 yd`

⑦ Sandy has $10.00. She gives $0.75 of it to charity. How much money does Sandy have left? `$9.25`

39

Be patient with your child as he or she is introduced to trickier subtraction problems. If he or she answers a question incorrectly, go through it step by step to make sure he or she understands where the mistake occurred.

42

① Multiply each number by 10.

5.0	`50`	7.5	`75`	8.6	`86`	0.3	`3`

4.2	`42`	0.8	`8`	7.1	`71`	5.7	`57`

7.44 `74.4`   9.25 `92.5`   3.09 `30.9`   5.12 `51.2`

3.17 `31.7`   0.71 `7.1`   8.54 `85.4`   0.89 `8.9`

2.645 `26.45`   7.321 `73.21`   76.342 `763.42`   41.545 `415.45`

② Multiply each number by 100.

3.4 `340`   6.8 `680`   7.1 `710`   5.2 `520`

6.0 `600`   2.7 `270`   9.9 `990`   1.01 `101`

8.27 `827`   4.86 `486`   12.7 `1,270`   13.1 `1,310`

5.887 `588.7`   5.854 `585.4`   34.22 `3,422`   75.734 `7,573.4`

43.882 `4,388.2`   33.297 `3,329.7`   423.67 `42,367`   123.78 `12,378`

③ Multiply each number by 1,000.

5.6 `5,600`   7.1 `7,100`   9.6 `9,600`   4.0 `4,000`

4.3 `4,300`   9.2 `9,200`   8.1 `8,100`   6.8 `6,800`

8.3 `8,300`   0.001 `1`   0.07 `70`   53.999 `53,999`

25.19 `25,190`   32.132 `32,132`   54.67 `54,670`   729.7 `729,700`

403.2 `403,200`   341.56 `341,560`   432.11 `432,110`   345.678 `345,678`

④ Write the answers.

320.006 x 10 `3,200.06`   32.143 x 100 `3,214.3`

29.15 x 1,000 `29,150`   201.12 x 10 `2,011.2`

17.487 x 1,000 `17,487`   56.195 x 100 `5,619.5`

121.165 x 100 `12,116.5`   782.01 x 1,000 `782,010`

812.84 x 100 `81,284`   297.49 x 1,000 `297,490`

253.786 x 10 `2,537.86`   723.707 x 10 `7,237.07`

43

Your child may have been taught some helpful tricks at school to solve this sort of multiplication. It is important for him or her to understand that when multiplying by 10, each number "grows," or is enlarged, by a factor of 10.

Answers:
44–45 Division and Rounding 1
46–47 Multiplication 2

44

① In what place is 7 in each of these numbers?

2.07	17.63	24.897	315.74
Hundredths	Ones	Thousandths	Tenths

7.12	12.37	70.139	29.871
Ones	Hundredths	Tens	Hundredths

② Divide each number by 10.

0.07 [0.007]   80.0 [8]   83.86 [8.386]   132.678 [13.2678]

24.8 [2.48]   63.96 [6.396]   4.331 [0.4331]   87.2 [8.72]

18.4 [1.84]   79.12 [7.912]   5.211 [0.5211]   325.986 [32.5986]

③ Divide each number by 100.

603.4 [6.034]   720.05 [7.2005]   3,300.8 [33.008]   200.005 [2.00005]

65.2 [0.652]   7,324.45 [73.2445]   723.966 [7.23966]   53.06 [0.5306]

6.45 [0.0645]   7.83 [0.0783]   34.32 [0.3432]   8.64 [0.0864]

45

④ Divide each number by 1,000.

6.3 [0.0063]   73.85 [0.07385]   923.357 [0.923357]   1,854.6 [1.8546]

0.4 [0.0004]   18.0 [0.018]   75.94 [0.07594]   50.67 [0.05067]

⑤ At the zoo, Eliza the Elephant weighs 8,250 lb. Billy the Bear is 0.1 (one-tenth), Chai the Cheetah is 0.01 (one-hundredth), and Polly the Penguin is 0.001 (one-thousandth) of Eliza's weight. How much does each animal weigh?

Chai the Cheetah [82.5 lb]   Polly the Penguin [8.25 lb]   Billy the Bear [825 lb]

⑥ Round each of these numbers to the nearest whole number.

66.67 [67]   3.52 [4]   253.91 [254]   504.54 [505]

25.35 [25]   4.15 [4]   621.32 [621]   698.35 [698]

48.01 [48]   3.89 [4]   481.69 [482]   523.78 [524]

A clear understanding of what dividing by 10, 100, and 1,000 actually means will help a great deal.

These pages also include extra practice in place values and rounding to the nearest whole number.

46

① Write the answers.

4.2 x 6 = [25.2]   2.6 x 8 = [20.8]   3.1 x 2 = [6.2]

5.9 x 6 = [35.4]   9.6 x 8 = [76.8]   1.8 x 9 = [16.2]

3.8 x 7 = [26.6]   6.6 x 4 = [26.4]   2.9 x 8 = [23.2]

4.7 x 9 = [42.3]   5.98 x 5 = [29.9]   7.13 x 6 = [42.78]

8.15 x 7 = [57.05]   3.65 x 4 = [14.6]   9.64 x 2 = [19.28]

4.56 x 3 = [13.68]   8.24 x 2 = [16.48]   9.66 x 4 = [38.64]

5.69 x 3 = [17.07]   8.64 x 7 = [60.48]   7.04 x 5 = [35.2]

3.08 x 9 = [27.72]   7.68 x 6 = [46.08]   8.98 x 9 = [80.82]

0.65 x 5 = [3.25]   1.06 x 7 = [7.42]   6.74 x 7 = [47.18]

9.81 x 7 = [68.67]   8.07 x 8 = [64.56]   9.36 x 4 = [37.44]

8.05 x 3 = [24.15]   1.09 x 6 = [6.54]   9.99 x 5 = [49.95]

47

② Solve these multiplication problems.

6.23	7.98	8.56	2.66
x 12	x 18	x 24	x 31
74.76	143.64	205.44	82.46

4.07	3.82	9.27	6.07
x 52	x 68	x 42	x 64
211.64	259.76	389.34	388.48

9.99	5.08	1.92	4.15
x 85	x 59	x 13	x 16
849.15	299.72	24.96	66.4

7.19	1.39	2.81	7.75
x 19	x 14	x 37	x 45
136.61	19.46	103.97	348.75

③ Simone gets $3.55 as allowance every week. Charlie gets $16.50 each month. Who gets the most in a year?

Charlie

As with so much of mathematics, instant and quick recall of times tables is essential. If your child is having trouble, ask them to work out an estimated answer before solving a question. It will take only a couple of seconds, and it can really help if the answer is a long way off.

Answers:

48–49 Division
50–51 Division and Rounding 2

48

① Write the answers.

$6.4 \div 8 =$ [0.8] $\quad 9.6 \div 8 =$ [1.2] $\quad 7.2 \div 9 =$ [0.8]

$0.4 \div 4 =$ [0.1] $\quad 1.7 \div 10 =$ [0.17] $\quad 0.3 \div 10 =$ [0.03]

$4.9 \div 7 =$ [0.7] $\quad 0.36 \div 2 =$ [0.18] $\quad 0.72 \div 12 =$ [0.06]

$4.2 \div 10 =$ [0.42] $\quad 0.48 \div 6 =$ [0.08] $\quad 0.36 \div 4 =$ [0.09]

$0.75 \div 5 =$ [0.15] $\quad 1.08 \div 9 =$ [0.12] $\quad 1.21 \div 11 =$ [0.11]

$0.54 \div 6 =$ [0.09] $\quad 7.28 \div 8 =$ [0.91] $\quad 8.19 \div 9 =$ [0.91]

$4.97 \div 7 =$ [0.71] $\quad 2.46 \div 6 =$ [0.41] $\quad 4.84 \div 4 =$ [1.21]

② Emily, Tom, and Sky have a yard sale and make $152.25. The money is divided equally between five charities. How much does each charity receive?

[$30.45]

49

③ Write the answers.

$4.32 \div 9 =$ [0.48] $\quad 13.8 \div 6 =$ [2.3] $\quad 27.3 \div 7 =$ [3.9]

$16.3 \div 5 =$ [3.26] $\quad 32.8 \div 4 =$ [8.2] $\quad 77.4 \div 9 =$ [8.6]

$64.6 \div 8 =$ [8.075] $\quad 48.1 \div 5 =$ [9.62] $\quad 81.9 \div 9 =$ [9.1]

$87.5 \div 7 =$ [12.5] $\quad 29.7 \div 4 =$ [7.425] $\quad 46.8 \div 4 =$ [11.7]

$89.7 \div 3 =$ [29.9] $\quad 93.5 \div 2 =$ [46.75] $\quad 69.3 \div 3 =$ [23.1]

$88.4 \div 4 =$ [22.1] $\quad 12.99 \div 6 =$ [2.165] $\quad 16.56 \div 8 =$ [2.07]

$28.15 \div 5 =$ [5.63] $\quad 22.76 \div 4 =$ [5.69] $\quad 39.12 \div 3 =$ [13.04]

$53.92 \div 8 =$ [6.74] $\quad 63.27 \div 9 =$ [7.03] $\quad 61.12 \div 8 =$ [7.64]

$53.12 \div 8 =$ [6.64] $\quad 76.44 \div 6 =$ [12.74] $\quad 72.36 \div 4 =$ [18.09]

$75.45 \div 5 =$ [15.09] $\quad 72.24 \div 6 =$ [12.04] $\quad 60.41 \div 10 =$ [6.041]

$80.15 \div 7 =$ [11.45] $\quad 102.2 \div 7 =$ [14.6] $\quad 104.8 \div 2 =$ [52.4]

Here, times tables knowledge is essential once again. Have your child make a quick estimate of the answer by rounding the figure. For example, $\frac{2}{10}$ can be thought of as $\frac{1.9}{8}$, giving an estimate of 0.2 with the exact answer 0.23.

50

① Solve each problem. Round the answer to the nearest penny.

$7 \div 3	$15 \div 7	$31 \div 5	$47 \div 3
[$2.33]	[$2.14]	[$6.20]	[$15.67]

$18.50 \div 3	$2.43 \div 6	$7.42 \div 9	$7.32 \div 4
[$6.17]	[$0.41]	[$0.82]	[$1.83]

$0.75 \div 4	$1.50 \div 7	$3 \div 9	$2.99 \div 4
[$0.19]	[$0.21]	[$0.33]	[$0.75]

② Solve each problem. Round the answer to the nearest centimeter.
(Hint: 100 cm = 1 m)

9 m ÷ 7	16 m ÷ 6	45 m ÷ 4	69 m ÷ 2
[129 cm]	[267 cm]	[1,125 cm]	[3,450 cm]

7 m ÷ 3	26 m ÷ 4	69 m ÷ 5	72 m ÷ 7
[233 cm]	[650 cm]	[1,380 cm]	[1,029 cm]

3.6 m ÷ 5	4.28 m ÷ 3	12.65 m ÷ 6	7.4 m ÷ 3
[72 cm]	[143 cm]	[211 cm]	[247 cm]

12.9 m ÷ 8	8.12 m ÷ 5	18.8 m ÷ 6	25.6 m ÷ 7
[161 cm]	[162 cm]	[313 cm]	[366 cm]

51

③ Solve each problem. Round the answer to the nearest gram.
(Hint: 1,000 g = 1 kg)

4 kg ÷ 6	19 kg ÷ 9	23 kg ÷ 12	12 kg ÷ 7
[667 g]	[2,111 g]	[1,917 g]	[1,714 g]

4.7 kg ÷ 6	11.9 kg ÷ 9	18.4 kg ÷ 7	16.9 kg ÷ 3
[783 g]	[1,322 g]	[2,629 g]	[5,633 g]

④ Solve each problem. Round the answer to the nearest meter.
(Hint: 1,000 m = 1 km)

2 km ÷ 3	17 km ÷ 8	38 km ÷ 6	33 km ÷ 5
[667 m]	[2,125 m]	[6,333 m]	[6,600 m]

1.78 km ÷ 4	2.06 km ÷ 9	3.63 km ÷ 5	20.4 km ÷ 7
[445 m]	[229 m]	[726 m]	[2,914 m]

⑤ Solve each problem. Round the answer to the nearest milliliter.
(Hint: 1,000 ml = 1 l)

8 l ÷ 6	13 l ÷ 4	40 l ÷ 7	46 l ÷ 8
[1,333 ml]	[3,250 ml]	[5,714 ml]	[5,750 ml]

23 l ÷ 9	43 l ÷ 5	62 l ÷ 3	17 l ÷ 8
[2,556 ml]	[8,600 ml]	[20,667 ml]	[2,125 ml]

Pay extra attention to the units in these questions; a question may be set in kilometers, but the answer may be required in meters. Remind your child of the coversions—for example, that 1 km = 1,000 m.

Encourage your child to use a calculator to check his or her answers after he or she has completed these pages.

Answers:

52–53 Division and Rounding 3
54–55 Decimals and Percentages 1

52 | **53**

① Figure out each answer and round to the nearest dollar.

$17.89 ÷ 3	$26.50 ÷ 4	$30 ÷ 7	$37.15 ÷ 6
$6	$7	$4	$6

$275 ÷ 3	$723 ÷ 6	$26 ÷ 6	$295 ÷ 4
$92	$121	$4	$74

② Solve each division problem. Round the answer to the nearest meter.

34.8 m ÷ 7	41.9 m ÷ 7	60.34 m ÷ 4	28.4 m ÷ 3
5 m	6 m	15 m	9 m

2,364 m ÷ 7	406 m ÷ 14	3,186 m ÷ 12	5,123 m ÷ 11
338 m	29 m	266 m	466 m

③ Solve each problem and round the answer to the nearest inch.

253 in ÷ 7	412 in ÷ 7	372 in ÷ 5	789 in ÷ 7
36 in	59 in	74 in	113 in

89 in ÷ 3	142 in ÷ 7	56.86 in ÷ 4	14.19 in ÷ 5
30 in	20 in	14 in	3 in

④ Solve each problem and round to the nearest gram.

43 g ÷ 2	317 g ÷ 6	500 g ÷ 6
22 g	53 g	83 g

534 g ÷ 7	250 g ÷ 9	890 g ÷ 12
76 g	28 g	74 g

⑤ Do each division problem and round to the nearest penny.

$2 ÷ 3	$53.60 ÷ 7	$120 ÷ 11	$28.30 ÷ 9
$0.67	$7.66	$10.91	$3.14

$85.62 ÷ 4	$49.12 ÷ 6	$59.52 ÷ 3	$72.12 ÷ 8
$21.41	$8.19	$19.84	$9.02

⑥ Solve each division problem and round to the nearest liter.

582 l ÷ 5	20.16 l ÷ 3	324 l ÷ 6	429 l ÷ 7
116 l	7 l	54 l	61 l

456 l ÷ 5	63.85 l ÷ 3	10.02 l ÷ 6	256 l ÷ 7
91 l	21 l	2 l	37 l

These calculations can take a long time, more than ten minutes. Have your child show their work, and then suggest they check their answers using a calculator. Remind them to be very careful with the units being used.

54 | **55**

① What is 70% of each amount?

$6	$23	6.5 ft	37 ft
$4.20	$16.10	4.55 ft	25.9 ft

② Write each decimal as its percentage equivalent.

0.75	0.45	0.333	0.125
75%	45%	33.3%	12.5%

0.01	0.9	0.375	0.3
1%	90%	37.5%	30%

③ Write each percentage in its decimal form.

55%	25%	12.5%	5%
0.55	0.25	0.125	0.05

65%	40%	80%	95%
0.65	0.4	0.8	0.95

④ What is 35% of each amount?

6 ft	4 mi	$12	7 ft
2.1 ft	1.4 mi	$4.20	2.45 ft

⑤ What is 5% of each amount?

$16	200 ft	$4.60	60 ft
$0.80	10 ft	$0.23	3 ft

⑥ What percentage of 200 is each of the following?

50	10	75	150
25%	5%	37.5%	75%

⑦ What percentage of 500 cm is each of the following?

50 cm	20 cm	25 cm	2 m
10%	4%	5%	40%

⑧ What percentage of $5 is each of the following?

$1	$3	$4.50	$0.10
20%	60%	90%	2%

⑨ What percentage of 150 is each of the following?

30	15	45	90
20%	10%	30%	60%

By this time, your child should have a good understanding of percentages and decimals and the relationship between them. This will help him or her develop quick and accurate methods for solving problems such as these.

Answers:

56–57 Decimals and Percentages 2
58–59 Estimation and Rounding

56

1. A highway was originally 40 mi long but has had its length increased to 60 mi. By what percentage has the highway increased in length?
   50%

2. David usually receives $5 allowance per week, but on his tenth birthday, his parents raised the amount by 10%. How much weekly allowance will David receive now?
   $5.50

3. Sean measured himself on his ninth birthday and was 45 in tall. On his tenth birthday he measured himself again, and this time he was 54 in tall. By what percentage has Sean grown?
   20%

4. A container carries 2,000 new TVs. When it is opened, 5% of the TVs are found to be broken. How many TVs are not broken?
   1,900 TVs

5. Emmie usually spends $80 a week on food shopping. Before the holidays, she increased this amount by 25%. How much money will Emmie spend per week now?
   $100

57

6. Victoria sends 500 texts per month. While on vacation, this number decreases by 70%. How many texts does Victoria send while on vacation?
   150 texts

7. A television show lasts for one hour, but 0.125 of this time is taken up by commercials. How long is the show without the commercials?
   52.5 minutes

8. What percentage of $1,000 is $50?
   5%

9. The area of a soccer field in a stadium is 8,000 m². After alterations, the area is reduced by 15%. What is the new area of the field?
   6,800 m²

10. An amount of money is increased by 35% and is now $27. How much was the amount before the increase?
    $20

These questions are put into realistic situations and require your child to figure out the operations needed to solve each one. Your child must read each question very carefully to see exactly what is being asked.

58

1. Round each amount to the nearest 10 dollars.

$12,753	$27,056	$70,000.24	$38,005.18
$12,750	$27,060	$70,000	$38,010

2. Round each amount to the nearest 100 dollars.

$51	$62,348	$92,062	$72,858
$100	$62,300	$92,100	$72,900

3. Estimate the answers. Answers may vary.

10.18 × 12	42.7 × 15	0.23 × 49	37.1 × 18
120	645	11	670

1.66 × 6	4.94 × 9	56 × 0.8	7.9 × 12
10	45	45	95

650 × 0.6	412 × 0.8	1,329 × 0.2	2,153 × 0.5
390	330	265	1076

6.82 × 7	2.19 × 8	37 × 0.9	56 × 1.8
48	18	33	100

59

4. Round each amount to nearest kilogram.

12,481 g	26,099 g	245,034 g	45,108 g
12 kg	26 kg	245 kg	45 kg

5. Round each distance to the nearest kilometer.

6,783 m	15,480 m	274,199 m	482,715 m
7 km	15 km	274 km	483 km

6. The cost of a cell phone is $480. During a sale, it is sold for $360. By what percentage has the price been reduced?
   25%

7. Copper piping is sold in lengths of 2.35 yd. A plumber needs 15 yd of piping. How many lengths will he need?
   7 lengths

8. Gas at a gas station costs $3.36 per gallon. How many whole gallons will $20 buy?
   5 gallons

Your child can work out his or her own estimation methods. Depending on the method he or she chooses, the answers may vary. The answers here are only generalizations of what should be expected.

Answers:

60–61 Solving Problems 1

62–63 Solving Problems 2

64–65 Beat the Clock 3, see p.80

60

① Which is larger, 30% of $20 or 15% of $50?

15% of $50

What is the difference between the two amounts? | $1.50

② Which is longer, 20% of 180 m or 45% of 400 m?

45% of 400 m

What is the difference between the two lengths? | 144 m

③ Which weighs more, 18% of 3 lb or 12% of 4 lb?

18% of 3 lb

What is the difference between the weights? | 0.06 lb

④ In minutes and seconds, how much is 12.5% of 1 hour? | 7 minutes 30 seconds

⑤ A plane trip is 7.5 hours long. If 80% of the trip has already passed, how much more time will it take to complete the trip? | 1.5 hours

61

⑥ Divide 6% of 300 by 0.4 of 30. | 1.5

⑦ Susan gives 10% of her salary to charity each month. If Susan is paid $1,780 each month, how much will she give to charity each year? | $2,136

⑧ What amount is...

... 15% less than $500? | $425

... 45% more than $5,000? | $7,250

⑨ What percentage of...

... 84 is 21? | 25%

... 400 is 20? | 5%

⑩ Fill in the boxes.

Reduce 4 mi by 2%. | 3.92 mi

Increase 6 lb by 3.5%. | 6.21 lb

Here, your child is provided with word problems to understand decimal calculations in real life. He or she must read the question very carefully to ensure he or she is giving the answer correctly.

62

① Which number is 60% more than each of these?

180	340	750
288	544	1,200

② What is 0.01 of each amount? Write your answers in dollars.

$12	$250	$800
$0.12	$2.50	$8

③ When a number is multiplied by 1.78, the result is 21.36. What is the number? | 12

④ Solve these riddles.

40% of a number is 12. What is the number? | 30

36% of a number is 72. What is the number? | 200

70% of a number is 98. What is the number? | 140

0.7 of a number is 14. What is the number? | 20

0.3 of a number is 5.4. What is the number? | 18

0.2 of a number is 2. What is the number? | 10

63

⑤ If a van travels at an average speed of 34.8 mph, how far will it travel in 5 hours? | 174 miles

⑥ Figure out the answers.

If 64 is 0.8 of a number, what is the number? | 80

What is 0.72 of 119? | 85.68

If 35 is 0.5 of a number, what is the number? | 70

What is 0.29 of 520? | 150.8

⑦ Nola usually scores 80 out of 100 on math tests. After studying very hard, her score goes up by 15%. What is Nola's score now? | 92

⑧ At the beginning of the year, a gold coin cost $450. By the end of the year, its cost went up by 25%. What is its cost at the end of the year? | $562.50

These questions mainly include operations like multiplication and division. Some of these calculations are fairly tricky. You should encourage your child to think them through carefully.

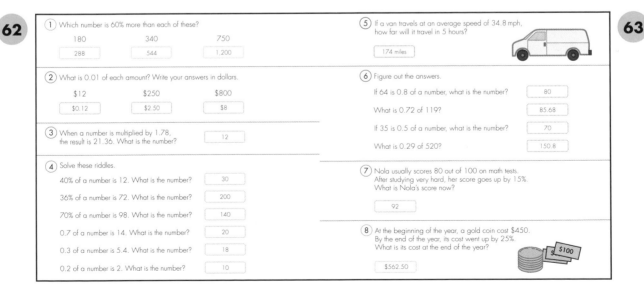

Answers:

20–21 Beat the Clock 1

40–41 Beat the Clock 2

64–65 Beat the Clock 3

These "Beat the clock" pages test your child's ability to quickly recall the lessons learned. The tests require your child to work under some pressure. As with most tests of this type, tell your child before he or she starts not to get stuck on one question, but to move on and return to the tricky one later if time allows. Encourage your child to record his or her score and the time taken to complete the test, then to retake the test later to see if he or she can improve on his or her previous attempt.

20 / **21**

(1) 0.25	(2) 0.75	(3) 0.5
(4) 0.4	(5) 0.8	(6) 0.2
(7) 0.6	(8) 0.9	(9) 0.1
(10) 0.7	(11) 0.4	(12) 0.5
(13) 0.6	(14) 0.8	(15) 0.3
(16) 0.7	(17) 1.8	(18) 1.2
(19) 2.1	(20) 0.2	(21) 0.5
(22) 1.1	(23) 3.0	(24) 5.0
(25) 0.6	(26) 40.0	(27) 15.0
(28) 36.0	(29) 70.0	(30) 49.0

(31) 5.67	(32) 4.97	(33) 1.64
(34) 8.52	(35) 12.97	(36) 1.35
(37) 8.05	(38) 9.43	(39) 0.66
(40) 7	(41) 8	(42) 3
(43) 8	(44) 8	(45) 10
(46) 22	(47) 37	(48) 4
(49) $\frac{75}{100}$	(50) $\frac{96}{100}$	(51) $\frac{2}{100}$
(52) $\frac{25}{100}$	(53) $\frac{675}{1,000}$	(54) $\frac{8}{1,000}$
(55) $\frac{30}{100}$	(56) $\frac{3}{1,000}$	(57) $\frac{5}{10}$

40 / **41**

(1) 9.1	(2) 5.9	(3) 10.6
(4) 12.9	(5) 10	(6) 9
(7) 9	(8) 8	(9) 11.2
(10) 14.1	(11) 7.5	(12) 6.6
(13) 6.5	(14) 10.9	(15) 6.1
(16) 1.7	(17) 5.1	(18) 12.7
(19) 7.4	(20) 10.46	(21) 1
(22) 3.1	(23) 7.77	(24) 10.61
(25) 12.94	(26) 8.42	(27) 9.21
(28) 11.72		

(29) 4.8	(30) 5.7	(31) 1.2
(32) 9	(33) 3.2	(34) 6.8
(35) 7.1	(36) 1.1	(37) 6
(38) 13.7	(39) 1.1	(40) 2.2
(41) $1.25	(42) $12	(43) $4.75
(44) $0.80	(45) 1.8 m	(46) $0.21
(47) 0.12 m	(48) $0.32	(49) $1.95
(50) 0.5	(51) 0.1	(52) 0.7
(53) 0.15	(54) 0.05	(55) 0.45
(56) 0.9	(57) 0.34	(58) 0.01

64 / **65**

(1) 75.0	(2) 168.0	(3) 0.3
(4) 709	(5) 2,405	(6) 306
(7) 500	(8) 3,880	(9) 100,100
(10) 0.46	(11) 6.01	(12) 10.3
(13) 0.16	(14) 42.5	(15) 0.3005
(16) 43.967	(17) 132.9	(18) 78.519

(19) 4.89	(20) 6.89	(21) 8.01
(22) 17.01	(23) 31.42	(24) 24.44
(25) 65.01	(26) 80.01	(27) 236.99
(28) 2.875	(29) 0.556	(30) 1.001
(31) 52.050	(32) 6.351	(33) 28.689
(34) 1.2	(35) 14.4	(36) 4.8
(37) 13.5	(38) 15	(39) 300
(40) 15.2	(41) 1.4	(42) 0.09
(43) 6	(44) 0.28	(45) 18
(46) 0.25	(47) 180	(48) 225